CALIFORNIA'S DEADLIEST WOMEN

Dangerous Dames and Murderous Moms

CALIFORNIA'S DEADLIEST WOMEN

Dangerous Dames and Murderous Moms

David Kulczyk

CRAVEN STREET BOOKS

Fresno, California

Published by Craven Street Books
An imprint of Linden Publishing
2006 South Mary Street, Fresno, California 93721
(559) 233-6633 / (800) 345-4447
CravenStreetBooks.com

Quill Driver Books and Colophon are trademarks of
Linden Publishing, Inc.

ISBN 978-1-61035-280-2

135798642

Printed in the United States of America
on acid-free paper.

Library of Congress Cataloging-in-Publication Data on file.

This book is dedicated to James A. Kulczyk.

Acknowledgments

I would like to thank April Moore, who edited this manuscript, and whose humor, skills, and grace guided me through the creation of this book. I would also like to thank Lorraine Clarke, Richard Sinn, James Van Ochten, Monica Downs, Mark Staniszewski, Tobi Shields, Amy Scott, Dana Wackerly, Brian Crall, Lisa Tuttle, Joan Renner, Jackie Koppell, John Massoni, Joseph Palermo, Theo Dzielak, Martin Imbach, Roberta Greene, Sherilyn Powell, Jody Marx, Marta Trevino, Esty Randolph, Angela Larson, Bob Pfeifer, Marilyn Sterrett, Michael Perry, Daniel House, Jen Picard, Rebecca Perry Damsen, Michelle Kapp, Becky Hoffman, Grant Eckman, Jessica Ashley, Bob Perry, Lisa Manzer, Joe Piecuch, Diane Parker, Jack Stanis, Jeff Engelstad, Avery Cassell, Michael Ravage, Eric Cooley, Eric Bergland, Mik Nei, Bill Forman, Sun Sachs, Michael Galligan, Carol Christopher, and William Burg. And, as always, I thank my wife Donna for giving me the time, space, and patience to do this project.

Contents

Introduction

Women have been called the "gentler sex," and for the most part this is true. We don't think of women as killers, we think of them as life givers and nurturers, so when a female does kill, it shocks us. In California, murderesses are so rare there are fewer than a hundred documented cases. I did not write about every woman murderer in California, because, frankly, most cases are not interesting.

It may seem that California has more murders than anywhere else, but according to the Death Penalty Information Center report of 2013, California ranked twenty-first in the United States with murder rates at 4.6 per 100,000 people. The estimated 2014 population of California was 38.8 million people. You have a better chance of being a murder victim in twenty-one other states. As of 2016, there are twenty women on California's Death Row. Out of those, eleven are Caucasian, six are Hispanic, two are Asians and two are African-Americans.

There are few heroes in this book and no happy endings. These cases are so bizarre, so puzzling, so corrupt, so disgusting, so gory, so inhumane, and so despicable, you will never forget them.

For this collection of crimes, I created some rules. I left out poisoners and child killers. I omitted females who were taking orders from their male counterpart. No Manson Family members in this book. Angels of Death were of no interest to me as the crimes were not violent. I wanted to write about the woman murderer who got her hands bloody, who left a mess. She had to commit the murder herself. Many women, who have been charged with murder, have an accomplice or two who did the dirty work. Of the four females officially executed by the State of California—Barbara Graham, Juanita Spinelli, Louise Peete, and Elizabeth Ann Duncan—only Peete did the actual killing.

Juanita Spinelli, who I wrote about in *Death in California: The Bizarre, Freakish, and Just Curious Ways People Die in the Golden State*, led a gang of young thieves in San Francisco and ordered the murder of gang member Robert Sherrod after he witnessed the accidental murder of a robbery victim and could not stop talking about it. With San Francisco police searching for them, the gang fled town and hid out in a Sacramento hotel.

Spinelli spiked Sherrod's drink with a narcotic and, after he passed out, had her minions beat him to death in their hotel room. They dumped him in the Sacramento River, hoping the strong current would carry him far downriver. Instead Sherrod's body got hung up on pilings, and was fished out of the river the next day. The gang was caught near the Nevada state line after Albert Ives, the man who killed the robbery victim and murdered Sherrod, realized that he was going to be Spinelli's next victim and called the police.

Louise Peete was a lifelong con artist, prostitute and thief. According to legend, Peete killed oilman Joe Appel in Waco Texas around 1912, but was acquitted because she claimed Appel sexually assaulted her. Aside from some early newspaper rumors and speculation, no other documents could be found to support this story. Also according to the legend, Peete left a trail of ex-husbands and lovers who committed suicide after she left them. I only authenticated one suicide attributed to Peete's aptitude for making her discarded lovers kill themselves. Peete served prison time for the 1920 murder of Jacob Denton, a wealthy Los Angeles mining engineer. She was released in 1939 to the custody of social do-gooder Jessie Marcy, who had lobbied the prison system for her release. Peete worked for Marcy as her caregiver and housekeeper until Marcy died of natural causes. Peete's probation officer, Emily Latham, took her in until Latham died of a heart attack in 1943. Peete married her fifth or sixth husband, Lee Borden Judson, a much older man who worked as a banker, and moved in with Arthur and Margaret Logan, a wealthy couple who had cared for Peete's daughter while Peete was incarcerated. Peete was to be the caregiver to Arthur, who suffered from Alzheimer's disease. Once Peete settled in, she shot Margaret in the head and buried her in her yard. She put Arthur in a mental hospital and started spending the couple's money. Judson did not know his wife had been in prison, and had no idea what she had done to the Logans. When police arrested Peete for Margaret Logan's murder, Judson committed suicide by jumping off the roof of an office building.

Barbara Graham is one of the saddest instances of an innocent person being condemned to the gas chamber. She was a third-generation Oakland prostitute who grew up in foster homes. As an adult she took up the family business to support her and her husband's heroin addictions and was at the wrong place at the wrong time with the wrong people. She was framed for a murder she did not commit. The mother of three was executed on the testimony of career criminals and murderers, Jack Santo and Emmett

Perkins, who went into the gas chamber a few hours after Graham. Santo and Perkins were the leaders of a murder/robbery gang that operated in Northern California for almost twenty years.

Elizabeth Ann Duncan, a drifter, bigamist, and prostitute, was deeply devoted to her son, Frank. Her life revolved around him, even as he grew up and became an attorney in Santa Barbara. He made her proud, except when he secretly married Olga Kupzyck, a nurse. She wanted her boy all to herself, even though he was twenty-nine years old. Duncan was desperate. She hired a man to portray her son, while she posed as Olga, and appeared in court to have the marriage annulled. Her scheme backfired when the clerk remembered the real couple. When Olga became pregnant, Duncan could not handle it. She hired twenty-five-year-old Augustine Baldonado and twenty-two-year-old Luis Moya, two inept hitmen, to murder her daughter in-law. They tricked Olga, who was seven-months pregnant, telling her Frank was drunk and they needed her to help him out of the car. Moya clubbed her on the head with a .22-caliber pistol. They tied her up with rope and tape and drove down the coast. They originally planned to dump her body in Mexico, but the men decided that Ojai, in Ventura County, was far enough. Dumping Olga down a culvert in the mountains outside of town, and intending to shoot her, Moya discovered he broke the gun when the beat Olga with it. Moya and Baldonado took turns choking the poor woman until they thought she was dead. The two dug a shallow grave with their bare hands. Olga's autopsy disclosed she had been buried alive. Elizabeth Ann Duncan was the last female executed in the state of California. Moya and Baldonado sat down in the same gas chamber before the seat was cold.

Why were Graham, Peete, Spinelli, and Duncan sentenced to death, while other female murderers were sent to prison? What all four women had in common is they were all unconcerned with the moral values of the times and comfortable with their sexuality. Peete was allegedly married six times, Graham five, Spinelli twice. And Duncan possibly wed over twenty times. Judges and juries saw them as hooch-drinking, dope-taking loose women with sticky fingers and homicide on their minds. While that is true, three of the four technically did not kill anyone and certainly did not deserve to be executed.

There are a number of murderous Californian females that deserve to be included in this book, however I have written in-depth about them previously, and felt it would be redundant for readers. Here is a summary of some of the deadliest California women not included in this book:

DOROTHEA PUENTE—1982–1988 (DATES OF CRIMES)

Dorothea Puente, a lifelong con-artist, whose final scam ended with at least six residents of her Sacramento boardinghouse dead. Puente laced selected boarders' food to knock them out so she could easily suffocate them with pillows. She had a simpleton handyman dig their graves in her midtown Sacramento yard. Puente then would cash their monthly social security checks at a nearby bar.

EDNA FULLER—AUGUST 30, 1926

San Franciscan Edna Fuller, not wanting to have her poverty-ridden family broken up and sent to orphanages, put her five children, who ranged in ages two to ten, to bed, sealed up the windows and doors to her drafty semi-basement apartment and turned on the gas from her oven. Father and husband. Otto Fuller found them all dead when he came home from his night job.

MARGARET ROWNEY—DECEMBER 14, 1950

Margaret Rowney, twenty-seven-year-old widow and mother of four, took her brood on a midnight drive on December 14, 1950. In a quiet spot in Topanga Canyon, under an ancient oak tree, Rowney taped a vacuum cleaner hose to the exhaust pipe of her Packard woodie wagon and inserted it though a partially open rear window. The family was found a few hours after the car ran out of gas. Rowney's thirty-six-year-old live-in boyfriend, Raymond Bennett, committed suicide the next day, the same way, in the same vehicle.

IDA BREWER—1853 AND 1855

Ida Brewer was a Sacramento prostitute with a quick temper. In 1853, Brewer stabbed and killed a rival lady of the night. A jury acquitted her of that murder, but two years later, using the same Bowie knife, she slashed the throat of a customer and shot another man in the chest. Brewer was found guilty, fined, and told to leave Sacramento.

JOSEFA—1851

The oldest known murder committed by a woman in California happened on the morning of July 5, 1851, in Downieville, a remote mining town in the Sierra Nevada Mountains. Drunken miners had filled the town on Independence Day to celebrate the seventy-fifth anniversary of the United States. Around seven in the morning, three intoxicated miners, Frederick

Cannon, Charley Getzler, and a man only known as Lawson, wanted to get the party started again and began pounding on doors and walls of the slipshod structures that passed as dwellings. When the drunken men came to the hovel where a gambler only known as José and his wife Josefa lived, the miners knocked the door off the hinges. The drunks stumbled inside the sleeping couple's home and started a commotion. Words were exchanged, and the men left, drunkenly putting the door back in its sill. A couple of hours later, Jose saw Cannon at a nearby barbershop and confronted him, demanding payment for a new door, and Cannon called Josefa a whore. However, feeling regret for being jerks to one of the few females in the entire state, Cannon and Lawson walked back to Jose and Josefa's shack to apologize. Josefa pulled out a huge Bowie knife and stuck it into Cannon's chest. He died where he fell. Josefa was grabbed by a crowd of angry miners on a three-day binge and put on trial. The miner's court assigned an attorney to represent Josefa, but the crowd shouted him down, pulled him out of the make-shift courthouse, and beat him to a pulp. Josefa was found guilty, and the mob took her to the bridge that crossed the Yuba River. When asked if she had any final words, Josefa replied, "Nothing, but I would do the same again if I were provoked." She asked for a proper burial, and shook hands with the men closest to her. "*Adios, señor*," she said to each of them. She threw her hat to a friend and put the noose around her neck. She hung for twenty-two minutes before being cut down and buried.

PENNY BJORKLAND—FEBRUARY 1, 1959

Teenager Penny Bjorkland had wanted to kill someone for a couple of years. The strawberry-blonde, freckle-faced eighteen-year-old found her victim on a beautiful winter day in the San Bruno Mountains, not a mile from her family home in Daly City. Using a stolen .38-caliber revolver, she shot random victim August Norry eighteen times. Norry, a married Korean War veteran who was wounded in action, worked as a landscape architect at the Lake Merced Country Club. He was also an expectant first-time father. He had been in the San Bruno Mountains to dispose of lawn clippings from a freelance gardening job that he took to earn more money. He was found lying next to his late-model Chrysler Imperial. Police thoroughly investigated Norry's background, expecting to discover a jilted lover. They were dismayed by a lack of motive. Only because of the determination of San Mateo County Sheriff's Department detectives Milt Minehan and William Ridenour was the case solved. Minehan and Ridenour determined the bullets dug out of Norry's body were special blunt-nosed wad-cutters used by target shooters who load their own bullets. The detectives traced the manufacturer of the bullet mold and narrowed down who purchased one in the Bay Area. Four months after August Norry's cold-blooded murder, the police discovered the purchaser was a twenty-three-year-old mechanic from Daly City. He told police he had sold a box of fifty wad-cutters to a pretty local girl, Penny Bjorkland. When the detectives went to the Bjorkland family home, they found a normal working-class family. Penny immediately admitted to murdering Norry, telling police, "Suddenly, I had the overpowering urge to shoot him. I kept shooting, emptying my gun and reloading. That was the only reason. There was no other." Penny Bjorkland pleaded guilty to second degree murder, served six years before she was released, and disappeared from history.

I wanted to capture the worst of the worst, the sickest of the sickos, the baddest of the bad, the most senseless, insane, idiotic, selfish murders committed by females in California that I could find. In these chapters you will read about women without conscious, without mercy.

With the exception of Swedish-born murderer Annika Östberg, it is unlikely any of the killers in this book— those who are still alive—will ever get out of prison. They will never know freedom again. Their lives will be sullen and gray until they die. They will live frozen in time, seeing the latest technical developments on television in the rec-room. They will never feel the happiness of holding a child.

This book was by far the most joyless project I have ever worked on. There is not one happy ending in any of the chapters. Just female criminals, who are selfish individuals, who are jealous, greedy, and do not have a single redeeming attribute among them.

Teenage Satan Worshipper

February 2, 1981—6330 Havenside Drive, Sacramento
Murderer: Kimberly Goytia
Victim: Stephanie Goytia

Kimberly Goytia did not fit the typical cliché of the California girl. She dressed in black and claimed to have worshiped the devil since she first saw the horror film *The Omen* in 1976. She collected and read books about Satanism and the Black Mass. Her mother, step-father, and eleven-year-old sister, Stephanie, did not think much about Kimberly's obsession. She was thirteen, a perfectly normal age for teens to act out in attempts to distinguish themselves from their schoolmates and family. For many, it is a passing phase, but Kimberly wanted to make it a reality.

February 2, 1981, was a Monday. The weather was cloudy and drizzling, just the way Kimberly would have liked it. Kimberly and Stephanie stood outside on the driveway to their apartment building where they lived at 6330 Havenside Drive, in the Greenhaven Pocket neighborhood of Sacramento. Back from school, they waited for their mother, Carol Summers to come home. The sisters had to kill time until then. Social options were few to preteens in the pre-internet era, and standing around in front of your driveway was one way to watch the world pass by.

Suddenly and without warning, Kimberly pulled out a .32 caliber semi-automatic pistol that belonged to her step-father and fired two shots at her sister.

One bullet entered her right arm and the second went straight into her heart. Stephanie fell screaming on the sidewalk next to a parked car, and bled to death. Kimberly walked back to the family apartment and called her uncle, who lived a few miles away, and told him what she did. When he got to the scene, he found Stephanie covered in blood. He called the police, as did neighbors who heard the shots and Stephanie's dying screams. They arrived to find the young girl lying face up, her adolescent features so bloody the police originally thought she was shot in the head. They arrested Kimberly and placed her into juvenile custody.

Sacramento County Deputy District Attorney Steve Secrest wanted to throw the book at the sibling-killing Satanist. At the time, a rash of crimes

was blamed on Satanism, and it appeared that Secrest had all of his guns on this case. He interviewed the Goytia family, schoolmates, teachers, friends and neighbors about Kimberly's fascination with the occult and the *Omen* films and books. Laughably, Secrest pointed out Kimberly had only worn black clothing for the last six months, going as far as retrieving them out of the garbage after her mother threw them away. Defense attorney Betty Rocker opposed the interviews and called them irrelevant hearsay intended to sway the court. Superior Court Judge Mamoru Sakuma dismissed the murder charges because the prosecution had failed to show malice. Kimberly Goytia was charged with manslaughter. In hindsight, it appeared that Secrest relied too much on the films, books, and Kimberly's inclination to wear black clothing.

The case went to Juvenile Court, where a recently-passed state law was enforced that protects juvenile criminals from media coverage unless they are charged with murder. On April 20, 1981, Superior Court Judge Mamoru Sakuma found Kimberly Goytia guilty of involuntary manslaughter. The thirteen-year-old was taken into the custody of the California Department of Corrections and Rehabilitation–Division of Juvenile Justice for an unknown period of time, and was ultimately released back into society without a word to the press.

The Evil Twin

March 19, 1950—4721 Harvey Avenue, Fresno
Murderer: Alice Richards
Victim: Sally Richards, Alice's twin sister

Fourteen–year-old Alice Richards was sick of her cheerful and vibrant twin sister Sally. The fraternal twins had argued earlier in the day over the use of the family telephone. Alice became furious when she was physically restrained by her sixteen-year-old brother Edgar. She threatened to shoot Sally with a gun, a threat serious enough to thirteen-year-old brother Robert, who hid the family's .22 caliber rifle. Horseplay, arguments and yelling isn't unusual in large families like the Richards', and after a few hours all seemed forgotten so Robert put the rifle back in its usual place.

Later that Saturday, Alice went to the neighbor's home where Sally was babysitting and stayed with her until the adults came back, around 2 a.m. Back at home, Sally fell asleep quickly, but Alice laid in bed still fuming. She crept around the house and got the rifle, put it to Sally's head, and fired the weapon.

Alice coldly walked to the family telephone, the very telephone they had earlier fought over, and called the Fresno Police. She told the dispatcher there had been a murder at 4721 Harvey Avenue. Her mother, Mary, woke up when she heard Alice talking to the police. Mary told the dispatcher she thought her daughter had a nightmare and that she'll check to see if anything was wrong. She came back on the telephone hysterically telling the dispatcher that her daughter Sally was bleeding.

Alice immediately told stunned Fresno police officers she had shot her twin sister. When the officers asked her why, Alice replied, "I hated her because she was always stupid and loud and acted like a nut."

In custody, Alice showed no remorse about murdering her sister. The bobbed-nosed Alice resembled the early Barbie dolls by Mattel. When she was brought into juvenile court, she smiled at photographers and people in the seats, but shunned her mother. She acted like she did not have a care in the world. When the court offered her the chance to attend Sally's funeral mass and burial, she refused. She assumed she would be put in a mental hospital, and eventually executed.

After hearing psychiatrists, juvenile authorities and attorneys report on the case, Fresno County Juvenile Court Judge Arthur C. Shepard ruled the blue-eyed, blonde sophomore would be committed to a state hospital for an undetermined amount of time.

"I don't feel bad because my sister is dead, but I feel bad for my folks. This'll hurt them. I'd kill Sally again if I had the chance." —Alice Richards

One Mean Swede

April 30, 1981—San Francisco
May 2, 1981—Middletown, Lake County
Murderer: Annika Östberg
Victims: Joe Torre and Sergeant Richard J. Helbush

Most immigrants to the United States come here for a chance at a better life, whether it is financially, socially, or religiously. Annika Östberg was not one of those émigrés. Born in 1954 near Stockholm, Sweden, she left the country at age eleven after her divorced mother married American Braxton Pollard III. They moved to St. Louis, Missouri. Östberg knew barely any English and struggled to get along with her step-father. Within a year Östberg landed in juvenile detention, which only hardened her. In 1967, at the age of thirteen, Östberg left home with a musician and headed off to San Francisco during the Summer of Love.

The hippie scene in San Francisco soon turned sleazy as the criminal element discovered how naïve the love children could be, and marijuana, hashish, and LSD was replaced with speed, downers, and heroin. Östberg became one of the many Haight Street casualties, when at an age she should have been taking driver's training classes in high school, she instead fell into an addiction to heroin. She also stripped in seedy nightclubs and prostituted herself to support her habit. She supposedly straightened out enough in 1970 to give birth to a son, Sven Johnson. It is unclear if Östberg married the father, but by 1971 she was back on the gritty streets of 1970s San Francisco, living with an ex-con named Chris Greenfield.

In 1972, when she should have been graduating high school, Östberg and Greenfield lived at 1000 Judah Street in San Francisco. Trouble broke out when another couple, sharing Apartment 303, were moving out. When twenty-four-year-old Donald McKay went back to the Judah Street apartment to retrieve his stereo, an argument ensued, and Greenfield stabbed McKay to death in the living room. There is doubt Greenfield did the actual stabbing. Some believe Östberg did the killing, and twenty-six-year-old Greenfield took the blame. Östberg received five-years of probation, probably because the police, district attorney and judge all believed Östberg

really committed the murder, but were unable to prove it. Why she was not deported at this time is unknown.

Over the next decade, Östberg allegedly married Brian Deasy, a truck driver, and the pair lived in Stockton, but Östberg could only commit to a life of crime. She went back to San Francisco and picked up where she left off, peddling heroin, committing misdemeanors, and working in the sex trade.

On April 30, 1981, Östberg and her latest criminal junkie boyfriend, Bob Cox, conjured up the brilliant idea of luring retired restaurateur Joe Torre to an isolated warehouse with the promise of selling him stolen meat. Fencing stolen meat to restaurants was one of Östberg's many criminal endeavors, and she had previously sold Torre purloined meat. Once inside the warehouse, Östberg led Torre to her truck to show him the meat she had to sell. Cox, who was supposed to be along for the ride, fired a bullet into the back of Torre's head, killing him. They took Torre's money and drove off to score heroin. The next day, in her heroin-soaked brain, she decided it would be a good idea to visit her son Sven, who lived with his father in Lake County, ninety miles north of San Francisco

Lake County has a rugged geography, with several fault lines and extinct volcanos covering the sparsely populated rural county. The county is dominated by Clear Lake, the largest lake completely in California. The huge fresh water lake, which at its broadest point is nineteen miles across, has long been a popular area for San Franciscans to vacation. Large weekend homes line the shore and the surrounding hills. On August 14, 1964, rockabilly legend Johnny Burnette died in a boating accident there.

Around midnight on May 2, 1981, the vehicle Cox and Östberg drove got a flat tire near Manning Flat on Highway 29, between the county seat of Lakeport and the village of Lower Lake. Thirty-four-year-old Lake County Deputy Sheriff Sergeant Richard J. Helbush pulled up behind the couple to offer assistance, but received three bullets in his back and one in the head for his efforts. Forensic evidence indicated that Östberg pulled the trigger. Stealing his wallet, gun and police car, the despicable couple left the deputy lying in a ditch on the side of the highway.

It is impossible to know what Cox and Östberg thought as they spent the night driving around the backroads of Lake County in a stolen police car. It is entirely possible they were so loaded on heroin that they were, in fact, not thinking, which eventually led to their capture.

When Sgt. Helbush failed to call in his location report at the scheduled time, a search for him began. They found his bullet-ridden body fairly quickly and soon every police agency in Northern California was on the lookout for the murderous pair.

Around daybreak, Lake County reserve Deputy Don Anderson and an off-duty California Highway Patrol officer spotted the stolen police car and gave chase. Cox only made it a short distance when he lost control of the car at the intersection of Dry Creek Cutoff and California Highway 175, near Middletown.

With the crashed police car on its side, Cox used it for cover as he shot it out with the two officers. Ever the badass, Östberg reloaded the guns for him while bullets flew. More police arrived and Cox, bleeding from two gunshot wounds, surrendered. Östberg was captured reaching for a pistol.

After the preliminary hearing, William Cox, believing he had a suicide pact with Östberg, hung himself in the tiny Lake County Jail. He had once served a prison sentence in Turkey and chose death over bars. This gave Östberg an opportunity to shift all the blame to Cox. She told police about her life of crime, which she attributed to her heroin addiction. Oddly, the blood sample they took out of Östberg had no traces of narcotics in it. However, drug testing was not as accurate in 1981, and it is possible that the test was botched somewhere along the chain of custody.

Östberg pleaded guilty to both counts of murder and was sentenced to twenty-five years to life in prison, and while there was little sympathy for the lawbreaking Swede in the United States, Östberg became a cause celeb in her native land. The Swedish media presented Östberg as a victim of the American justice system where drug addicts are left to their own devices and fall into a life of crime. The lack of drug rehabilitation for the users as well as the conditions of the prisons in California was politely pointed out. The death of her son Sven in a Napa County automobile accident in 1985 helped her cause, even though she barely had anything to do with the raising of Sven.

Eventually, the government of Sweden got involved and started the diplomatic procedures to have Östberg released to Swedish authorities so she could finish out her sentence in the civilized prison system in their county, where books and plays were written and performed about her. A Swedish television documentary that depicted the Lake County Sheriff's

Department as ignorant thugs did nothing to make the parole board reduce Östberg's sentence.

She was denied parole in 1997, 2002, 2005, and 2008, but because of the media attention from Sweden, along with quiet pressure from the Swedish government, Östberg was let out of the California Institution for Women in Chino on March 25, 2009, and into Federal custody. By April, she boarded a private airplane chartered by the Swedish government and flew back to her homeland. At fifty-seven, she was detained at the Hinseberg Women's Prison where she was coddled and rehabilitated into Swedish culture. Officials even allowed her out of the prison to be interviewed on television and radio programs. On May 2, 2011, Annika Östberg, a woman without any socially redeeming qualities and responsible for at least four murders, was released after thirty years of imprisonment.

The Bad Detective

February 24, 1986—7100 Balboa Boulevard #205, Van Nuys
Murderer: Stephanie Ilene Lazarus
Victim: Sherri Rae Rasmussen

As children, we are taught that the police are our friends and we can always go to a policeman if we are lost or in trouble. We are advised that the police are here to "Protect and Serve," but as we become older the police become more like a nuisance than a protector. Cops seem to love to dole out undeserving traffic tickets to young adults, or shut down parties right when the fun begins. When you reach middle-age the cops never seem to be where they are needed, except when handing out a traffic ticket. Most of us rarely have contact with a police officer, and when we do, it is usually not under the happiest of situations.

A lot of corny prose has been written about "what is a cop." From pioneer television cop Jack Webb to the self-righteous radio commentator Paul Harvey, it is forever popular to remind the public about the ridiculousness of what is expected of a cop. How they are supposed to remain calm and professional while a hyped up hoodlum is screaming insults about their mother's sexual habits, or how cops risk their lives every day for people they do not know. A police officer is expected to not show emotions when holding the lifeless body of a child, or when giving CPR to a heart attack victim until an ambulance arrives.

Sherri Rae Rasmussen was a twenty-nine year-old newlywed living with her husband, John Ruetten, in their condominium at 7100 Balboa Boulevard in Van Nuys. John worked as a mechanical engineer and Rasmussen had a job as a supervising critical care nurse at Glendale Adventist Medical Center. Rasmussen was something of a wonder nurse, entering college at age sixteen, becoming a registered nurse at twenty, and then a high ranking nurse before she turned thirty.

On February 24, 1986, Sherri had a sore back from doing aerobic exercises and stayed home from work. Sometime during the morning, after John left for work, one or two persons broke into their home and a struggle between the intruders and the athletic Sherri Rae ensued, resulting in Sherri getting shot three times in the chest with a .38 caliber pistol. John

Ruetten discovered his wife's body when he came home for work around six in the evening. He immediately called the police.

Los Angeles in 1986 was in the grips of a crime wave, and detectives were overburden by their workload. To the police, the crime looked like a burglary gone wrong. Daytime is a favorite time of day for burglars, as they can be fairly sure no one will be home, but a startled burglar can panic and resort to violence.

That is what Detective Lyle Mayer concluded: a burglar broke into the condo expecting the occupants to be away at work, and was surprised by Sherri. A physical confrontation occurred upstairs, and Sherri was carried down into the living room where she was hit in the head with a vase. Rasmussen was almost six-feet tall, and fit. She had put up a good fight, and at one point during the struggle the killer had bitten her on her left inner forearm as if they were in a headlock or struggling over the gun. It appeared at this point the burglar shot Sherri point-blank in the midsection with a Smith & Wesson .38 caliber snub-nosed pistol. She was tied up and wrapped in a blanket before she was shot two more times in the chest, again at point-blank range. The burglar or burglars left a stack of stereo gear by the door, but did take Sherri's purse, BMW automobile, and, oddly, the couple's marriage certificate.

Detective Mayer quickly cleared John Ruetten as a suspect. He believed it was a simple burglary gone wrong. He neglected to interview neighbors, or Sherri's coworkers and friends. He ignored Ruetten when he told them they should question a former girlfriend, Stephanie Ilene Lazarus, a Los Angeles police officer.

Sherri's parents arrived from Phoenix the next day and told the detective their daughter had recently told them she was being stalked by a woman with crazy eyes who wore a hooded sweatshirt. Sherri's friends and coworkers also knew she was being followed and harassed by the patrol officer. She told them Lazarus would appear out of nowhere when Sherri was at the grocery store, restaurants, or the gym. Lazarus went as far as going to Sherri's workplace to confront her about her marriage to Ruetten, telling her, "If the marriage doesn't work out, I want you to know that I'll be there to pick up the pieces."

Even armed with this information from five different sources, Detective Mayer stuck to his theory that Rasmussen was the victim of an interrupted burglary and refused to question Lazarus. His theory was reinforced when three weeks later another burglary was interrupted at the condo complex and witnesses described two Hispanic males fleeing the scene.

The case petered out from there. Detective Mayer got abrupt with Rasmussen's family when they called for updates in the case. The murder devastated John Ruetten, who moved to San Diego and eventually remarried. In 1996, ten years after her murder, Sherri's father, Nels Rasmussen, offered to pay for a then-brand-new and costly DNA test. The L.A.P.D. turned him down.

Stephanie Lazarus was born in Southern California in 1960, and grew up into an athletic California girl. She attended U.C.L.A. with John Ruetten. They lived in the same dorm and were both active in intramural basketball. The two would often have casual sex with one another, but did not have a romantic relationship. When Lazarus graduated in 1982, she surprised her family by entering the Los Angeles Police Academy. John Ruetten got a job at an engineering firm and widened his social circle, meeting and falling in love with the engaging Rasmussen. Once the word got out among the old college gang that Ruetten was in a serious relationship, Lazarus reacted with uncharacteristic anger. No one thought her anger and frustration with someone who was a casual college sex partner would lead to murder.

Lazarus was a sharp beat officer and she quickly rose through the ranks of the L.A.P.D., becoming the police's representative of the failed Drug Abuse Resistance Education program, also known as D.A.R.E. She also served as treasurer of the Los Angeles Women Police Officer's Association for five years. Officer Lazarus was always willing to help out with fundraisers. During a time when police agencies all over the country were scrambling to hire female officers, Lazarus was the L.A.P.D.'s dream officer. She was, as the old cliché goes, "a cop's cop."

In 1996, she married fellow L.A.P.D. officer Scott Young. The couple adopted an infant daughter and lived in Simi Valley, which had become a suburb popular with law enforcement officers. Young was stationed in the San Fernando Valley before being promoted to detective, while Lazarus continued on as an instructor until 2006, when, at 45, she took a position with the LAPD's two-detective Art Theft Detail, the only full-time unit of its kind in the country.

By 2008, the crime wave in Los Angeles had crested, leaving quite a few detectives sitting around playing trash can basketball. The department beefed up the Cold Case Detail to keep the experienced detectives from being laid off or bumped back down to uniformed officers. In February 2009, the unsolved case of Sherri Rae Rasmussen landed on the desk of the cold case crew, led by Detective Rob Bub and including Detectives Jim Nuttall, Pete Barba, and Marc Martinez.

The sloppiness of the 1986 investigation stunned the crew and they were flabbergasted to realize one of their own, a member of the L.A.P.D., was mentioned as a potential suspect. To make matters even more fraught, that suspect was now a highly respected detective who had an office just down the hall from theirs. They saw Detective Lazarus in the busy hallways of the Parker Center on an almost hourly basis. They knew they had to work in secret on this case, as Lazarus had a lot of friends on the police force and if any word got out to her before the detectives were ready, the case could be sabotaged. Lazarus was known in the department as a clever cop who strategically planned her moves. The cold case squad gave Lazarus the code name "Five," and kept the file under lock and key. They did not even inform their supervisors about the case or who their suspect was.

The detectives learned Lazarus had owned a .38 caliber revolver at the time of Rasmussen's murder. It was a personal gun, not her service pistol issued by the department. More intriguing, Lazarus reported the gun stolen three weeks after the murder. It further intrigued the crew that she went out of her way to the Santa Monica L.A.P.D. precinct to report the stolen gun. Since she worked for the police department and was at their station house five days a week, it would have been more convenient for her to report the theft at her own precinct. It appeared Lazarus was attempting to avoid suspicion.

The best piece of evidence in the case was a swab taken from the bite wound on Rasmussen's left inner forearm. DNA identification was in its infancy when Rasmussen was murdered, but one crime scene investigator had enough foresight to collect the saliva around the bite mark. The cold case crew sent the swab for DNA testing and waited for the results. The detectives were ecstatic when the DNA test came back positive for a female and not the male illegal aliens that Detective Mayer had claimed committed the crime in 1986.

The detectives needed to covertly obtain a sample of DNA from Lazarus. Undercover police officers tailed Lazarus when she was not on duty, hoping she would leave something with her DNA on it. After days of trailing Lazarus while she went about her daily chores, they caught a break. Lazarus had bought a soda drink in a shopping mall, and threw out the cup and straw after she finished it. The detectives snagged the cup and straw out of a trash bin and took it in for processing.

A few weeks later, the results came back. The saliva on the bite mark on Sherri Rasmussen's forearm belonged to Stephanie Ilene Lazarus. That meant the only suspect in the cold case was one of their own. The news came in May 2009, four months after Bub and the trio of detectives reopened the case.

With all the evidence needed to arrest Detective Lazarus, the team had to plan the best way to capture her. They had no way of knowing how she would react if she was armed when confronted with the evidence. She was not only a clever police officer, but also a cold blooded murderer, who thought nothing of killing an innocent person and then living a rich and rewarding life for over two decades without remorse. For safety reasons it is against L.A.P.D. policy for anyone to have a firearm on them in the interview rooms. They had to get the wily detective away from her minions and into an interview room where she would not have her sidearm with her.

June 5, 2009, was the last day Lazarus would wear a police officer's badge, but she did not know it at the time. The cold case detectives lured Lazarus to an interrogation room with the excuse they had a suspect who had information about one of her art theft cases. The detectives were polite to Lazarus, explaining they had a touchy situation. She seemed to immediately know something was up, and played dumb.

When questioned, Lazarus hemmed and hawed, trying to remember who John Ruetten was. Once reminded, she declared she barely remembered him because it was so long ago, and that she did not know him very well. Nervously, she started to bring up dates and life events, ridiculously adding and subtracting years. Lazarus had a hard time admitting she had dated and had a sexual relationship with Ruetten while in college. She pretended to only have a vague recollection of Sherri Rasmussen, claiming she could not remember ever having a conversation with the victim. She could barely recall meeting up with Ruetten while on vacation with friends in Hawaii in the late 1980s. She started a lot of her statements with "I would say," and ended a lot of her sentences with "I don't know" and "It was a million years ago." She peppered her answers with laughter and odd facial expressions.

When asked to submit a DNA sample, Lazarus balked and lawyered up. She was handcuffed discreetly in the hallway by waiting detectives as she left the interview, returned to the interrogation room and was read her rights. She acted as if this was nothing but a big mistake, and giggled, "No," when ask if she would like to speak to them without a lawyer present. While being lead out into the hallway she said, "This is crazy, I'm in like, in shock, I am totally in shock."

The trial started on July 21, 2012, twenty-six years after Sherri Rasmussen was found dead with three bullets in her chest in apartment 204 at 7100 Balboa Boulevard in Van Nuys. Deputy District Attorney Shannon Presby said in his opening statement, "The case against Lazarus came down to a bite, a bullet, a gun barrel, and a broken heart." Over the next five weeks the prosecution presented more than 60 witnesses and 400 exhibits. But DNA collected from the saliva on the bite mark on Rasmussen's left inner forearm that matched Lazarus's DNA proved to be the most damaging evidence—the odds of a faulty match were just one point seven sextillion to one.

Lazarus's attorney, Mark Overland, tried his best to prove his mugging and giggling client not guilty. He claimed the package containing the swab in a test tube was open, contaminating the evidence. Detective Lyle Mayer, now retired, was called to the stand to testify. He stuck to his original story; however, the jury did not believe him.

On March 9, 2012, Lazarus was found guilty of first degree murder. On May 11, 2012, a judge sentenced Lazarus to twenty-seven years to life. She is imprisoned at the Central California Women's Facility in Chowchilla, California. She will be eligible for parole in 2034.

Had it not been for the sharp investigation skills, determination, and fearlessness of Detectives Rob Bub, Jim Nuttall, Pete Barba, and Marc Martinez, the murder of Sherri Rasmussen would have never been solved, and bad cop Stephanie Lazarus would have gotten away with murder.

The Doctor's Wife, Part I

October 4, 1945—San Francisco
Murderer: Annie Irene Mansfeldt
Victims: Vada Martin and Dr. John Mansfeldt

San Francisco socialite and amateur actor Annie Irene Mansfeldt decided to finally confront Vada Martin over her longtime affair with her husband, Dr. John Mansfeldt, a prominent San Francisco physician. On October 4, 1945, she left her luxurious home at 2853 Vallejo Street and drove down the hill to downtown.

Annie had asked Martin, who was employed by Dr. Mansfeldt as a nurse, to meet her in her car on Van Ness in downtown San Francisco, near the doctor's office. The meeting did not go well. Mrs. Mansfeldt pistol whipped and then shot Martin, dumping her off at the San Francisco Receiving hospital, where she soon died.

Doctor Mansfeldt, who was a resident at the hospital, arrived and was informed that his wife shot his lover. Doctor Mansfeldt silently got into his car and drove away. He was found three days later, twenty miles down the coast from San Francisco, dead in his car of a morphine overdose.

After a painfully long trial, the thirty-six-year-old mother of three served twenty-five months in Tehachapi before was released back into society.

The Doctor's Wife, Part II

November 5, 1989—1041 Cypress Ave, San Diego
Murderer: Betty Broderick
Victims: Dan Broderick (ex-husband) and Linda Broderick (new wife)

Few murderers in modern history have caused as much controversy and publicity as Betty Broderick. Her story has been told in at least four books and countless magazine articles. Broderick has been interviewed on television shows like *Oprah Winfrey, 20/20,* and *Hard Copy*. In 1992, a two-part television movie (with the double title of *A Woman Scorned: The Betty Broderick Story* and *Her Final Fury: Betty Broderick, The Last Chapter*) garnered an Emmy nomination for the star, Meredith Baxter. The reason why Betty Broderick's crime was celebrated is because the man that she murdered, her ex-husband, attorney/physician Dan Broderick III, was a complete scumbag, unworthy of compassion. Betty may have gotten off with a very lenient sentence had she not also killed Dan's new wife, Linda.

Elizabeth "Betty" Broderick was born on November 7, 1947, to Frank and Marita Bisceglia. She grew up in Eastchester, New York, as the third of six children in a strict but loving home. Frank worked in his family's successful family business and their children lived in a nice house, complete with maids, went to good schools and grew up without want. Elizabeth grew up into a smart, five foot eleven, blonde beauty. She attended the College of Mount Saint Vincent in nearby Riverdale, New York.

In 1966, while attending college, she and a friend traveled to South Bend, Indiana to attend a chaperoned football weekend at Notre Dame University. At a party held for the students, she met pre-med senior Dan Broderick. Dan was celebrating his acceptance to Cornell Medical School. When he found out that Betty was from New York, he asked her if he could look her up when he got there. Betty thought it was funny that it appeared that Dan did not know that Cornell University was located in Ithaca, New York, 222 miles west and north of New York City. She gave him her contact information and, thinking that it was just party talk, she forgot about him once she got back home.

To Betty's surprise, she started receiving telegrams and long letters from Dan, and once he made his move to Cornell, he made plans to meet her

under the clock at Grand Central Station. Betty had a hard time remembering what Dan looked like, and was leery about going to Manhattan by herself, but she agreed to meet him. Dan showed up wearing a white lab coat, which thrilled the naïve Catholic girl.

On their third date, while Dan was driving Betty's MG around New York City, she suggested that they go visit some friends of hers. Dan pulled over the car and sternly told her that, "You don't tell me what we're going to do!" When she timidly asked what he wanted to do, he replied angrily, "You don't make the decisions, I do. That's my job."

Usually Dan treated Betty like a queen, a queen that he wanted to have as his own. But as their relationship progressed, Dan became more and more controlling. Instead of going home for the summer, he stayed in New York to keep an eye on Betty. He even stayed at Cornell over the Christmas holiday so that Betty could not date other men while he was gone.

Daniel Broderick III was born in Pittsburgh, Pennsylvania, on November 22, 1944. World War II was looking like it would be ending soon, with both Japan and Germany losing battles and consistently withdrawing from captured territory. Proud Irish Catholics, Daniel and Yolanda Broderick were overjoyed that their first-born child was a boy. In Junior's numbskull, drunken brain, males were everything; women on the other hand were servants and baby machines. Daniel Junior, the first member of his family to graduate from college and a naval officer during World War II and after the war, became a successful lumber salesman. He expected obedience from his family. It was forbidden to speak during dinner when Junior was there. His long suffering wife, Yolanda, was kept pregnant until she was physically unable to have children anymore. Nine children in total, and the daughters were treated as servants to the males in the family. The boys in the family all went on to college at Notre Dame and were expected to be the best at everything.

To Betty's New York friends and family, Dan was looked at as a semi-hick, over-dressed to impress, but ignorant of the big city. He was so full of himself that for Betty's nineteenth birthday he gave her a framed color photo of himself. He proposed to Betty while visiting his family in Pittsburgh.

They were married on April 12, 1969, at Betty's church, Immaculate Conception Church in Eastchester. Dan showed up with a huge hangover, and spent most of the ceremony trying not to throw up. After the lavish reception, paid for by Betty's parents, the couple flew to their honeymoon on the Caribbean island of Saint Thomas. Betty was alight with romance as she was a good Catholic girl; in other words, she was a virgin. Dan, who had been technically drunk for days, did not bother with any foreplay with Betty. He simply lifted her skirt, raped her, and passed out. He spent their vacation drunk and sullen.

Betty moved in with Dan in his small apartment that he shared with a roommate. Unknown to both of them, she had become pregnant over their honeymoon. Betty got a job as a school teacher, but on January 24, 1970, she went into labor. When Dan came home, he was drunk, and had brought home a fellow student and a prostitute. Dan passed out in the hallway of their apartment building while on the way to the hospital. Betty had to take a cab and delivered their daughter, Kim, before Dan woke up.

Betty found herself being a mother to both Kim and Dan, and as the bread earner of the family she had zero time for herself. She was looking forward to springtime, when Dan would graduate from medical school and they would have a somewhat normal life, perhaps in another city. Dan had other plans. Without Betty's knowledge, he applied and was accepted to Harvard Law School in the fall. He believed that being a physician and an attorney would earn him more money in the field of law. Dan got an internship in Pittsburgh where they lived with Dan's parents and their household of unmarried children. They moved to Cambridge, Massachusetts, in August to a basement apartment in a Portuguese immigrant neighborhood. Dan had picked out the place.

Betty picked up part-time jobs, and to makes ends meet they got by on food stamps. They had no car, although Dan had a motorcycle, so Betty had to take a bus during the bitter cold of a Boston winter just to go to a laundromat. She was in a no-win situation. By the time that Dan came stumbling into the apartment in the early morning hours, he was too drunk to have a conversation. When their second daughter, Lee, was born, Betty took a cab to the hospital, even though they by then owned a car. Dan had to study for an exam.

Taking a summer internship in San Diego, Dan uprooted the young family again. Betty got pregnant for the third time in as many years. The pregnancy was physically hard on Betty and she bled throughout it. Back in Boston, when the time came for the baby to be born, Dan was skiing in Vermont, and Betty gave birth alone. The baby died two days later. After the funeral, a distraught Betty tried to commit suicide by taking every pill in their home, but Dan ended up saving her.

After graduating from Harvard Law School in 1973, the family moved to San Diego, California, and Dan was quickly hired as an attorney at the prestigious law firm Gray Cary, Ames and Frye. Money was tight with two children and school loans to pay back, but Betty again took on a half-dozen part-time jobs to keep the family afloat. When Betty got pregnant again in 1973, she got an abortion, which was now legal, without telling Dan.

Drama could not stay away from the Broderick family. On Christmas Eve, while Dan and Betty were out doing last minute gift buying, their house caught on fire. The teenage babysitter got the girls out of the house, but the home was a total loss. Not only that, but Betty was pregnant yet again. Using the insurance money, they bought a house that was beyond their means in La Jolla. During their first winter in the house, they could not afford to heat the place.

Betty was back at work a couple of months after their first son, Daniel T. Broderick IV, was born. Her varicose veins from her multiple pregnancies made it impossible for her to do restaurant work anymore, so she started an informal day-care out of her home. Most of the mothers in the neighborhood would drop their children off while they treated themselves to lunch at a seaside restaurant and some clothes shopping.

In the meantime Dan was rubbing elbows with as many influential people as he could meet. He played tennis, had meetings in bars and restaurants. He was rarely home. Dan's mind was on making money, and to have a better life, but while he was out wining and dining clients, he was losing out on his family life. They both became passive-aggressive towards each other in public, with Betty correcting his grammar or poking fun of his Pennsylvania background.

Another baby was in the oven, and when Betty suddenly went into a bloody labor, Dan reluctantly drove her to the hospital, carefully placing towels on the car seat and floor so it would not get bloody. She gave birth to a boy they named Rhett. After many spirited discussions, Betty had her tubes tied. She was tired of being pregnant, and being ill. It took months for Betty to recover from Rhett's birth. Betty was angry that Dan had never once fed or changed any of his children. She was sick of him being gone all the time. She was even more tired of Dan coming home completely drunk in the early morning hours.

Dan felt that he was not getting paid what he was worth at Gray Cary, Ames and Frye. He was not only an attorney, he was a medical doctor who specialized in malpractice lawsuits. He decided to start his own law firm.

It was not long before Dan was amassing clients at his firm, and was soon making more money than he ever thought was possible. He joined the board of directors of the bar association, and became the go-to guy for personal injury and malpractice law. He had achieved all of his goals, and yet he was not happy. Always a dapper dresser, Dan had expensive suits tailormade. He bought expensive cars and was very peculiar that they were kept extraordinarily clean. Betty and he attended grand galas for various causes. He made sure that his father knew about his accomplishments, sending him newspaper clippings just to rub his nose in it.

Dan was still a drunk. He was still distant with his children. Even with all of his education, Dan had the mental maturity of a drunken twenty-year-old frat boy. He would drive home blitzed, bumping into trees and driving on the wrong side of the street. Often times Dan would pass out in his car after he parked it in their garage.

With all of his goals accomplished, and sitting on the top of the San Diego legal community, the last thought in Dan's head was to enjoy the fruits of his labor with his family. While Betty took the children on a lengthy multistate camping trip, Dan started an affair with a new office girl that he had recently hired.

Linda Kolkena was from a large close-knit Catholic family from Iowa. Born on June 26, 1961, she was seventeen years younger than Dan Broderick. Her mother died when she was a teenager, and she left the family home after her father remarried. At sixteen she lied about her age to become a flight attendant for Delta Airlines, but was fired for not only for being underage, but for allegedly having sex, in-flight, with a male passenger while intoxicated. She has blue eyes, blonde hair and high cheekbones. She was a younger version of the now thirty-five-year-old Betty, who despite having five hard pregnancies that wrecked her body was still a size eight. Like so many people who have never fit in, Linda Kolkena ended up moving to California around 1982, allegedly following a boyfriend who moved there.

While the family was on their summer tour of the American West, Dan purchased a nearby home for him and his new girlfriend to live in. Shortly afterwards, Dan left his family home. Expecting a brouhaha when Betty found out about his new living situation, Dan financially held all the cards.

The septic pool that was the Brodericks' relationship completely backed up. The tortured relationship between Betty and Dan turned toxic. Betty became obsessed with her anger towards Dan. She had left her big Italian family and a comfortable life with a bright future to working multiple menial jobs to put Dan through first medical school and then Harvard Law School—all the while pregnant and raising the children essentially by herself. There was supposed to be a payoff for all the sacrifices that she made, and all that she got was to be dumped for a younger woman. All the money, cars, clothing and jewelry could not make it up to the livid Betty Broderick. For Betty, none of these material things could compensate for all those days of working double shifts at restaurants. Nothing could make up for those long and painful pregnancies, the dirty diapers, the missed birthdays, the vacations ruined. In Betty's Catholic trained brain, marriage was a sacrament, something through which couples rode out the ups and downs of life together, until death do they part. The years of mental and physical abuse had forged Betty's mind like a blacksmith hammering on red hot metal. It could only be undone by completely destroying it.

For four years Dan, Linda, and Betty's lives would be filled with divorce proceedings, restraining orders, destruction of property, arrests, custody hearings, police calls, lawsuits, vandalism, obscene and threatening messages and involuntary stays in mental hospitals. The case garnered a lot of publicity as Betty use the abused spouse defense, an argument that had merit, but Dan entirely had the upper-hand in the case. He kept unemotional about the case, and gave Betty anywhere between nine and sixteen-thousand dollars a month. Allegedly Dan dragged the case on with legal maneuverings, and by the time the case went to court Betty had to represent herself. Dan, who was the president of the San Diego Bar Association, got the judge to close the court to spectators and even had the windows of the courtroom covered. The divorce proceedings lasted eight days, and when it was finally over, Betty ended up owing Dan over seven-hundred thousand dollars. To add salt to the wound, Dan got custody of their four children. Betty was devastated when the couple tied the knot on April 2, 1989.

On November 5, 1989, using her daughter's key, Betty slipped inside the newlywed's home. Standing at the foot of the bed, Betty pointed her Smith & Wesson .38 caliber pistol and fired all six bullets in the gun. Linda was hit in the upper-left chest and in the back of her head. Dan was shot in the chest, and had a slow and painful death. He would have bled to death had he not asphyxiated on his own blood first.

Betty called her daughter, Lee, and turned herself over to the police. Telling detectives she had planned on shooting herself, but was startled when Linda started screaming, she squeezed the trigger until the gun clicked on empty chambers.

Broderick retained the services of attorney Jack Earley, who used the battered wife defense. Years of mental, psychological and physical abuse by Dan pushed her over the edge. The prosecution argued Betty planned the murders, right down to unplugging Dan's telephone so he could not call for help. The prosecution pointed out that although the marriage had soured, her life was far from ruined. Betty resided in a half-million dollar beach house in tony La Jolla, owned two cars, and received sixteen-thousand-dollars a month in alimony. Her two sons lived with her, and she had a live-in boyfriend.

Her first trial ended with a hung jury, but she was retried a year later, found guilty of two counts of second degree murder, and sentenced to two consecutive terms of fifteen years to life. Betty has been behind bars since the day of the murders. Her sentence ends in 2021.

Not So Rosy

June 13, 1990—Hedlund Drive, Anaheim
Murderer: Maria del Rosio "Rosie" Alfaro
Victim: Autumn Wallace

To the millions of people who visit Anaheim every year, their only concern is to have a good time at the most famous theme park in the world, Disneyland. They want to forget the troubles of their lives, and the world, if only for a day. It is of little concern to them that outside their hotel window is a real place.

In the early 1990s, if you stepped outside the Disneyland grounds on South Walnut Street and West Audre Drive, you have a very good chance of experiencing a very bad time. Drugs, prostitution and robberies were so rampant in that area city officials changed the name of Jeffrey Street to Calle del Sol, just to confuse the drug addicts.

Maria del Rosio Alfaro, known to everyone on Jeffrey Street as "Rosie," became a neighborhood regular when she was twelve years old. Rosie grew up the daughter of an abusive drunk, was raped by a friend of her father's when she was nine years old, and dropped out of school in the seventh grade. Her father finally left his family for good when Rosie was twelve, but that did not bring any stability to her life. At a time when most girls her age were excited about a school dance, Rosie was shooting heroin and cocaine with Jeffrey Street denizens and prostituted herself to pay for it.

Rosie's mother, Sylvia, was only seventeen when she had Rosie. She worked at Disneyland, putting in as many hours as she could to provide for her family. She first became aware of Rosie's drug problems when Rosie was twelve. She claimed she had Rosie in a drug treatment program, but her insurance stopped covering the treatments after two weeks. Out of desperation Sylvia sent Rosie to live with her mother in Mexico, hoping her guidance and the new experience would snap young Rosie out of her need for drugs and the dirty culture that comes with it. Sylvia's mother sent Rosie back to Anaheim six months later. At fourteen, Rosie gave birth to her first child, Daniel.

Motherhood did nothing to stop Rosie's ride with the devil. Her drug of choice was the "Speedball," a mixture of heroin and cocaine. She liked

to inject it into her arms or neck. This same combination of drugs killed comedy star John Belushi in 1981. Sylvia would often find her out on the streets of Anaheim, barefoot and dirty, in a stoned-out stupor.

A second child, Manny, was born when Rosie was fifteen. There seemed to be no hope Rosie's life would be anything other than a long or short descent into narcissistic debauchery. To stay as high as Rosie liked to be, she engaged in sex acts with anyone who had the drugs or the money. Her very existence centered on injecting and procuring heroin and cocaine. She would disappear for days, only to show up at a friend's or relative's home or place of employment to ask for money. She looked like an extra from a Mexican vampire film, but was a walking, disease-spreading skank. She dressed uber-Chicana in tight black clothes, pancake make-up, long fake fingernails and brushed out hair. Her eyebrows were shaved and drawn on, and heavy eyeliner outlined her bottom eyelids. Multiple shades of red lipstick made her lips look otherworldly.

June 13, 1990, was a Friday, and Rosie, seven months pregnant with twins, wasted little time scoring dope that morning. She arrived at her dealer's place at 11 a.m. By two in the afternoon, Rosie ran out of dope and money. A friend, Antonio Reynoso, offered to share his drugs with her, if she would share her hypodermic needle with him. Reynoso, who had just been released from prison the day before, did not know what he was getting into when he decided to hang out with the eighteen-year-old Rosie. Once they went through Reynoso's drugs and were out of money, Alfaro had an idea, but she needed a ride and someone to watch one of her children. Reynoso and a man, who was never identified, agreed to help out. Reynoso would soon regret allowing himself to get involved.

Rosie told her friends she knew of a house only a few blocks away she could easily burglarize to get money for more drugs. Childhood friend April Wallace lived there with her small child, her mother Linda, and nine-year-old sister Autumn.

When Rosie was homeless and pregnant with her second child, Linda Wallace had showed Rosie kindness and let her live with them. April and Rosie eventually had a falling out in their friendship and rarely saw each other.

Forty-year-old Linda Wallace worked as a clerk at the Orange County Superior Courthouse. She had lost her husband, the father of her three children to cancer a few years earlier. Her oldest daughter, twenty-two-year-old Amber, had moved out on her own.

Rosie knocked on the door of the Wallace home and was greeted by Autumn, who had just gotten home from school and was waiting for her sister and mother to come home from work. Rosie asked to use their restroom, to which Autumn agreed. Little Autumn, an A student who loved to color and create art, went back to cutting out paper dresses. Rosie walked to the bathroom in the back of the house, eyeing over what she could steal along the way. Using an excuse that she needed help with an eyelash curler, Rosie called out to Autumn. While Autumn fiddled with the curler, Rosie used a paring knife she picked up in the kitchen on her way to the bathroom to stab the young girl. She did not stop until she had stabbed her over fifty times. Rosie quickly grabbed a television set and a VCR machine and took it out to the waiting car. Reynoso, who held Manny, and the unidentified man, stood outside the car in the driveway. Running back into the house, Rosie grabbed anything of value she could find. She took a typewriter, clothes iron, lamp, radio, calculator, a video game console, mirror, clock radio, clothing, and a pair of boots. She wanted to take the family's microwave oven, but ran out of room in the car. Reynoso and the unidentified man had no knowledge that Alfaro murdered the little girl inside the house. They drove off to sell or trade their ill-gotten loot for more heroin and cocaine.

When April Wallace came home from work around 5:15 p.m., she saw that the house had been ransacked, and waited outside until her mother came home from work. When Linda arrived she entered the house, saw the blood spattered walls and her butchered little daughter dead on the bathroom floor.

As police roped off the crime scene and homicide detectives started their investigation, a horde of neighbors and lookie-loos stood behind the police line, wondering what had happened. One of the rubberneckers was Antonio Reynoso, who still carried little Manny.

Neighbors told police they saw a brown or gold color Monte Carlo in the Wallace's driveway around three in the afternoon, and that two Hispanic men stood outside waiting.

Alfaro left over twenty bloody finger, palm, and shoe prints throughout the Wallace home. Detectives lifted a bloody fingerprint off the bathroom sink later identified as belonging to Alfaro.

Rosie Alfaro went to her friend, Maria Ruelas, and asked if she could leave a bag of clothes at her home. Alfaro and her boyfriend, Manuel Cueva, who was also the father of her children, would often rely on Ruelas for a place to stay when the wretched couple needed help. Alfaro told Ruelas she was leaving for Mexico the next day and would pick up the bag before she left. Detectives retrieved the bag on June 24, and upon opening it found it to be full of blood-soaked clothing.

The next day, police picked up Maria del Rosio Alfaro and brought her in for questioning. She folded like a cheap card table when asked about the murder of little Autumn Wallace, and told the detectives she committed the crime. The entire confession was recorded.

When her trial started, Alfaro started singing another tune. She claimed she was forced to commit the murder by a man, who she only knew as Beto. Alfaro claimed Beto said that Autumn Wallace had to be killed because she witnessed the burglary, and that he would kill her family if Rosie did not kill Autumn Wallace. No evidence supported Alfaro's allegations. Her defense attorney brought up some character witnesses for Alfaro, including a fellow drug-addicted prostitute who sickened the jury with her detailed descriptions of her and Alfaro's drug use and life as a prostitute.

Her other character witness was a manager of a fast food franchise where Alfaro once worked for a few weeks, the only legal job Alfaro ever had. Perhaps out of desperation, her attorney informed the court that his client had an IQ of only 78, which would put her in the category of mentally retarded. Her abusive, alcoholic father, tough upbringing, and failure at school were emphasized by her attorney as the reasons Alfaro went so far astray from the social norm. Finally, the mother card was played, as if Alfaro was even close to being a good mother.

The physical evidence against Alfaro was overwhelming. Her bloody fingerprints were all over the house. The bag containing her clothes had Autumn's blood on it, and Rosie's bloody shoe prints perfectly matched the ones she left at the murder scene.

On March 23, 1992, the jury, which took less than four hours to decide, convicted Alfaro of first degree murder. On July 14, 1992, Maria del Rosio Alfaro was sentenced to death. She is currently one of three females on California's Death Row. Oddly enough, getting the Death Penalty probably extended Alfaro's life longer than if she had stayed in the lifestyle she had been living before she so callously killed Autumn Wallace.

Batgirl

March 5, 1991—North Natomas, Sacramento
Murderer: Michelle Cummiskey
Victim: Philip Inhofer

Michelle Cummiskey did not have much of a chance in life. She had been mentally, physically, and possibly sexually abused during her childhood in New Liberty, Iowa. Running away from home at the tender age of fourteen, Michelle fell into the skin trade, where she spent the next six years as a dancer, stripper and prostitute in such wide-ranging places as Reno, Phoenix, Los Angeles, Illinois, New York, Florida, and Hawaii. At a time when most teenagers are concerned about acne, getting good grades, and going to the prom, the tall, green-eyed brunette spent these formative years ingesting drugs, dancing naked on stage and having sex with strangers for money. She married California businessman Jade Cabading, but their relationship was stormy at best. Without divorcing Cabading, Michelle married Jason Rush, who she met while stripping at a bar in Honolulu. That marriage did not last either.

At twenty years old, Michelle found herself working at the Mustang Ranch, the notorious legal Nevada brothel, while keeping a small apartment in Citrus Heights, a suburb of Sacramento. She decorated her flat with rubber bats and posters of vampire films. She had a series of especially vivid tattoos; a ring of bats in flight, as if coming out of a belfry, on her upper left arm, and vampire bite marks on her neck, complete with dripping blood.

Philip H. Inhofer was a retired Air Force veteran who lived in a trailer park in the North Natomas area of Sacramento. Like many veterans, he worked at nearby McClellen Air Force Base. Inhofer's Air Force pension, along with his civilian employee status at McClellen, provided a comfortable living for the five-foot-six grandfather. His red 1975 Mercedes Benz 450SL sport coupe looked out of place in the working class, semi-rural neighborhood. His two grown sons and their families lived nearby.

Inhofer struggled with alcohol. Once a square-dancing enthusiast, Inhofer backed away from his social life, and eased into his semi-retirement knowing that he was destined to spend his golden years living a

solitary life. He diminished his loneness by paying for escort services. His favorite call girl was Michelle Cummiskey.

For most people Tuesday is just another day to knock over the dominos of the week. A low-key day, when work gets done and nothing special happens. Unknown to Philip Inhofer, Tuesday, March 5, 1991, was the last day of his life.

Cummiskey spent the day with Inhofer. They went shopping at Target, but sometime during the evening hours something went violently wrong at the modest trailer home. After not showing up at his job at the air base on March 7, his employer notified Inhofer's son. He found his father, naked in the closet of his bedroom, beaten and stabbed over thirty times. A white garbage bag was tied around his head. The red Mercedes 450SL was missing.

The family told detectives that Inhofer was seeing a woman whom, he told his family, he was in love with. After a quick look at his phone records, police traced back a collect call. It turned out to be a man who let Cummiskey use his telephone after her car got stuck in the snow near Soda Springs. More of Cummiskey's "friends" came out of the woodwork with claims that she had planned to buy rat poison to kill Inhofer. Another person said she drove Cummiskey to Inhofer's home the day of the murder. She told police that Michelle, who claimed that she enjoyed running from the police, carried a pistol.

An unidentified Sacramento sheriff deputy admitted he had once had a sexual relationship with Cummiskey. Another source told police that Cummiskey told her she killed one of her husbands by dropping a radio into the tub while he bathed. All of these so-called "friends" were knee-deep in prostitution, drugs and other lowlife endeavors, and their statements could hardly be considered credible. But with not much else to go on, police put out an all-points bulletin out for Michelle Cummiskey, who the media labeled Batgirl, after her tattoos and goth rock looks.

For two months, a nation-wide search was on for Batgirl. Even the *Weekly World News*, a now defunct weekly tabloid full of ridiculous stories from dubious sources covered the story of the Batgirl. Television programs like *A Current Affair* and *Court TV* ran clips about her.

On May 7, 1991, a Biloxi, Mississippi police officer was making his rounds near the beaches of the Gulf of Mexico when he noticed the open rear door on a rental truck, parked on a beach access road. Inside the truck was a silver Mercedes 450SL. He thought that it was unusual to transport a car in the back of a truck and questioned the two occupants, who turned out to be Cummiskey and a friend, twenty-six-year old, Crystal Annette Li. The two were apparently on their way to Miami to work at a strip club when they were spotted by the officer.

The officer found a small amount of marijuana on the pair. He ran a warrant check and found that Chumminsky was the wanted Batgirl. She was arrested and held at the Harrison County Detention Facility in Gulfport on charges of murder and grand theft auto. Sacramento homicide detectives got on the first flight in the morning to make their way to Mississippi.

On May 13, 1991, television, radio and newspaper reporters, along with dozen of cameramen, waited at the Sacramento Airport for the exotic murderer with the name of a cartoon hero. They hoped to get a glimpse of her athletic build, blue-black hair, and heavily made-up eyes, not to mention the bloody vampire bite on her neck and the flying bats that danced on her left bicep.

Instead they saw a frightened twenty-year-old freckle-faced woman, who looked more like a college student than a murdering, coke-loving, weed-smoking, vodka-drinking, itinerant good-time girl. When Cummiskey saw the brigade of reporters and cameras, she leaned her head into her police escort's shoulder and broke into tears.

Cummiskey tried to explain what happened the night of Inhofer's murder the best her emotionally and intellectually-stunted brain could. She told police she had taken LSD, then took a shower with Inhofer. When the LSD kicked in, she thought Inhofer was the devil and that she had to slay him. She also thought Satan wanted her to be the best evil machine possible, and wanted to protect her. She stated she had lost her soul because she had hurt someone (Inhofer) she loved. Given the testimony of her "friends," her two ex-husbands, and a treasure trove of incriminating evidence—such as a ledger of her Johns, love letters from duped servicemen stationed overseas, and juvenile ramblings about cutting and killing people—Michelle Cummiskey faced a possible death sentence. In a plea bargain, she admitted to the murder of Philip Inhofer.

At the sentencing, Michelle Cummiskey wore a cotton dress with tiny purple and blue flowers on it. For the first time in years, her hair was its natural color of brown. Her curly long hair covered her vampire bite tattoos.

She could have easily been mistaken for a teenager in traffic court, but Cummiskey never had a chance to be a teenager. She never had a chance to be a child. The dysfunctional family life she endured as a child would never have allowed her to have a normal life.

While her former schoolmates were sneaking kisses on hay rides, Michelle was dancing topless at seedy strip clubs and selling sex acts to strangers. At a time when her ex-schoolmates were enjoying a keg and bonfire party in an Iowa farm field, Michelle was snorting foot-long lines of cocaine and wearing nothing but a smile. Back in Iowa, girls Michelle's age were going off to college and saying goodbye to their high school boyfriends, who they knew they would never see again, while Cummiskey was juggling a dozen different servicemen stationed overseas, getting as much money as she could hustle out of them, and working as a prostitute at the Mustang Ranch.

Addressing the court at her sentencing, Michelle "Batgirl" Cummiskey told the assembled in a Valley Girl accent: "I don't blame anybody for what happened to me, but I wish I would have been taught better. Nobody is born an evil person. We all have a spark of goodness, and if it's nurtured and developed, it can grow and chase away the blackness, the negativity that's out there."

As of 2015, Michelle Cummiskey is still serving her twenty-six-year sentence at the Valley State Prison for Women in Chowchilla, California.

Murder in Kings Canyon

September 18, 1955—Kings Canyon National Park
Murderer: Anna Guild
Victim: Charles Guild

Forty-seven-year-old Anna Guild and her husband, thirty-four-year-old Charles, ran a concession stand in Wilsonia, near the General Grant Grove in Kings Canyon National Park. Living among the giant trees would be a dream come true for most people, but once the tourist season ends the giant wilderness park can become a lonely place.

On September 18, 1955, Anna and Charles were drunk and arguing about their marriage when Anna picked up a .22 caliber rifle and shot Charles dead. She claimed it was an accident. Since Wilsonia is in Kings Canyon National Park, Anna's case went to Federal Court instead of to a county court, and after a four-day trial, a jury of ten men and two women found her guilty of involuntary manslaughter.

On January 3, 1956, Judge Gilbert H. Jertberg of The United States District Court, Eastern District of California, sentenced Anna to one year in federal prison. Apparently, the entire village of Wilsonia witnessed Charles' penchant for getting drunk and roughing up Anna.

Justice was served cold that January in 1956.

She's a Man Eater

November 28, 1991—Costa Mesa, Orange County
Murderer: Omaina Aree Nelson
Victim: William Nelson

Omaina Aree was born in Egypt in 1969, not a great year to be living in the Middle East as Egypt, Jordan, and the Palestinian state engaged in bloody warfare with Israel. There is not much information about Aree's life before she immigrated to America at eighteen, and what little that we do know is that the five-foot tall, well-endowed beauty was a victim of female genital mutilation as a girl in Cairo.

Being young and beautiful helped Omaina get a foothold in her new country, and it seemed she never lacked for male companionship. Because of her circumcision, sex was painful and traumatic, so she got her sexual thrills through bondage. One of her favorite bondage games involved tying up her middle-aged lover on a bed and leaving with his money and valuables. There are at least two cases where this was documented; however both men later refused to pursue the charges. Not many men are willing to testify in court that they were tied up, robbed, and who knows what else by a tiny exotic woman with the promise of kinky sex. Only Omaina knows how many times she pulled off that stunt.

Richard Nelson must have been different from the other men Omaina dated because the two married after knowing each other a few days. The large, fifty-six–year-old pilot from Costa Mesa, who was once convicted of drug smuggling, led the usual middle-age lifestyle of resignation and quiet desperation.

November 28, 1991, was Thanksgiving Day in the United States, and all around the nation, family and friends gathered together to eat and socialize. Richard and Omaina had plans for some bondage games. Omaina securely tied up her new husband to their bed, took a clothes iron, and beat Nelson over the head with it. Just to make sure that he was dead, Omaina used a pair of scissors to repeatedly stab Nelson in the chest. Already in the holiday spirit, Omaina dressed in her bondage clothes, put on red high-heel shoes, a red hat, applied blood-red lipstick, and started cutting up her dead husband.

Detectives showed up at Omaina's apartment on December 2 after one of her former boyfriends called the police informing them that Omaina asked him to help dispose plastic bags of leftover turkey and body parts. The detectives were sickened by the bloody mess they discovered. Nelson's head had been cooking in a pot on the stove. His hands were fried in cooking oil. Bags of Nelson's entrails and other body parts were found in the trunk of Nelson's red Corvette. She later told a psychiatrist that she had cooked his ribs, dipped them in barbecue sauce, and ate them. Omaina admitted to investigators that, "Nothing tastes as good as the man I married. It's the sauce that does it."

At trial, her attorney told the judge and jury about Omaina's traumatic childhood in Egypt, where she was not only a victim of female genital mutilation, but was also allegedly subjected to years of sexual abuse. He also claimed Nelson beat and raped Omaina and she was merely defending herself when she killed him and, in her psychotic state, butchered, cooked, ate, and disposed of his body parts. What the defense failed to explain was how Nelson was a threat to her when tied down to their bed. They also failed to thoroughly explain why Omaina butchered, cooked, and ate Nelson.

On February 26, 1993, Omaina was convicted of second degree murder and sentenced to twenty-eight years to life in prison. She was denied parole in 2011. Whatever nightmare upbringing that haunted Omaina in her young adulthood, the memory of butchering her husband and eating him will stay with her for a very long time.

Life of Crime

January 26, 1992—1123 Industrial Road, San Carlos
March 11, 1992—777 California Street, Palo Alto
Murderer: Celeste Simone Carrington
Victims: Victor Esparaz and Caroline Gleason

You would think that a name like Celeste Simone Carrington would belong to a person of royal blood, or at least rich East Coast stock, but Celeste Carrington was anything but royalty. She and her siblings were born poor and black in Philadelphia to parents who barely provided for them. When Celeste's mother would leave her children alone in their home for days without food, Celeste had to take care of her younger siblings, begging for food from neighbors and digging through garbage cans behind restaurants. When her mother was home, she beat Celeste and her siblings for any reason. Her father began raping her when she was seven years old and got her pregnant when she was fourteen. After getting an abortion, she left home.

Carrington spent the next sixteen years on the edges of society. Moving often, she worked menial jobs and, surprisingly, when considering her upbringing, stayed out of trouble. Either that or she never got caught. Somewhere along the line she earned her General Education Diploma and took some courses at a Southern California community college. Sometime in the early 1990s, she ended up in East Palo Alto, California.

East Palo Alto is not a prosperous place like the city to the west that shares its name. Until 1983, it was officially an unincorporated part of San Mateo County, and was technically an island dependent on county services with no city government. Prior to WW II, Japanese-Americans and other immigrants tended the farmland-rich area, but once the war began and those of Japanese heritage were relocated, the U.S. military used it as a training camp.

When the war ended, and along with it restrictions on building materials, cheap housing was built to relieve the Bay Area housing shortage. Racist real estate laws and the discriminating practice of banks redlining areas where they would not secure loans doomed East Palo Alto to become a city of claptrap apartments and rampant crime. In 1992, East Palo Alto

had the highest murder rate (172.7 homicides per 100,000 residents) per capita in the county. Overall, crime in the Bay Area was at an all-time high.

But Carrington's life was finally settling down. She shared an apartment with Jackie, a single mother of three whom she was madly in love with. Having to provide for herself, Jackie, and the children, Celeste worked for a janitorial company that serviced office buildings on the peninsula. However, she was fired in late 1991 when caught stealing checks. Carrington kept the keys of the buildings that she had cleaned, knowing they could come in handy at a later time.

With no money coming in to support Jackie and her brood, Carrington broke into a Dodge auto dealership in Redwood City on January 17, 1992, where along with cash and electronics she stole a loaded .357 Magnum pistol from an employee's desk.

On January 26, Carrington borrowed a neighbor's car and used her stolen keys to gain entrance to an office building at 1123 Industrial Road in San Carlos. When she tripped off the alarm, custodian Victor Esparaz approached Carrington. She told him she was also from the janitorial company and was scheduled to work there that night. When Esparaz let his guard down, Carrington pulled out the large pistol on him and took forty dollars that he had in his wallet, his ATM card and his personal identification number. She made him get down on his knees before shooting the thirty-four-year-old in the head.

Carrington was believed to have been involved in a dozen burglaries on the peninsula during the early months of 1992, all of them with the same method of operation. Using her stolen keys and a crowbar, Carrington would enter businesses that she used to clean and go through desks, looking for cash or anything of value.

On March 11, 1992, Carrington got a ride from a neighbor to 777 California Street in Palo Alto, to burglarize yet another building she had the keys to. The lock to the building had been changed, but Carrington saw two custodians inside and decided to wait until they finished before she would break in. Once the cleaning crew left, Carrington used a screwdriver to open the lock. The building was slim pickings for the thief, until she heard thirty-six-year-old property manager Carolyn Gleason enter the building. Ambushing her in a photocopy room, Carrington took four-hundred dollars, an ATM card and the car keys from the frightened woman. She forced Gleason to her knees and mercilessly shot her in the head.

Carrington took Gleason's car and drove to ATM machines to raid Gleason's bank account. Only two of the cash machines gave her money, and only a few hundred dollars. She ditched the car at a Palo Alto hospital and called a taxi to take her home to East Palo Alto.

Five days later, on March 16, Carrington went to another office building at 801 Brewster Avenue in Redwood City. She was surprised to find the building still open, so she hid in a closet to wait for everyone to leave for the day. After the building cleared out, Carrington attempted to enter offices she had the keys to, but none of the locks would open. Spotting Dr. Allan Marks alone in his office, Carrington burst through the door waving her gun. The young pediatrician recognized her from when she cleaned his building and put up a fight. During the struggle, Dr. Marks was shot twice with the large caliber bullets hitting him in the left shoulder, left thumb, and right forearm. Luckily for the doctor, the last bullet in the pistol misfired. Carrington managed to steal some sample drugs and access cards before Marks shoved her out of his office, locking the door and calling the police.

Amazingly, Carrington continued her burglary spree, possibly committing two more burglaries until the early morning hours of March 21, when police from Los Altos, Redwood City, and Palo Alto arrived with a search warrant at the apartment she shared with Jackie and the three children. The detectives found a staggering amount of evidence, including the keys Carrington failed to return, as well as Gleason's cash box, her PIN written on a piece of paper, and her purse. The police also found drug packets from Doctor Marks' office, and the .357 Magnum pistol, with spent shells still inside the cylinders.

The trial was an open and shut case with the evidence overwhelming the jury. Despite the public defender's plea to spare her the death penalty because of her horrible childhood, Celeste Simone Carrington was found guilty of the attempted murder of Dr. Allan Marks and guilty of the murders of Victor Esparaz and Carolyn Gleason. As of 2015, she is on San Quentin's death row.

The Shopping Spree Killer

February 14, February 28, and March 16, 1994—Canyon Lake
Murderer: Dana Sue Gray
Victims: Norma Davis, June Roberts, and Dora Beebe

Dana Sue Gray was born Dana Sue Armbrust to former fashion model Beverly (née Arnett) and hairdresser Russell Armbrust on December 6, 1957, in Orange County. Her birth was extremely special to the couple as Beverly miscarried twice before the zygote that would become Dana Sue managed to make its way to Beverly's uterus and grow into an embryo. Beverly already had two boys—ten-year-old Rick and eight-year-old Craig—and the happy family bought a home in Covina.

Beverly had a demanding and controlling disposition and had no problem enforcing her will on her family. She also had a taste for the finer things in life like clothes and jewelry. She spent more than they earned, and by 1959 her marriage was over.

Beverly practiced Scientology, and spent her money on the church's pricey classes. Her son, Craig, became a professional musician while still in high school and toured for extended periods of time. Beverly made ends meet by renting out a room in her home in Covina to a man who would soon become her lover. She also rented out the driveway to some men who lived in a recreational vehicle. Beverly liked to go nightclubbing with her girlfriends and she often had parties at her home. She did not set the best example for young Dana.

Growing up in Covina, Dana Sue often misbehaved at school and at home. She had an odd obsession with money, inexplicably knowing it had worth even as a toddler. She got into violent fights with other girls at school, shoplifted, and refused to take orders from anyone. She often sneaked out of her bedroom at night and wandered the streets in the dark. She lost her virginity at the age of twelve to one of the men who lived in the camper in her driveway.

Around 1971, doctors diagnosed Beverly with breast cancer. After seeing how her mother suffered while dying from cancer, and the callous treatment Beverly received from the nurses, Dana decided to take her studies

seriously and become a nurse. It was one of the few acts of empathy Dana Sue ever demonstrated in her entire life.

After Beverly died, Dana moved in with her father and his new wife, Yvonne, at his home in Dana Point. She shared a bedroom with Yvonne's daughter, Cathy, which did not sit well with Dana. Suffering the loss of her mother, she continued to be a high-spirited girl, testing the patience of her father and step-mother. Seeing she needed some kind of hobby, Dana's stepbrother Rick took her skydiving. She took to her sport with gusto, quickly becoming an expert jumper. The exhilaration of free-falling out of an airplane provided a good stress release. After two years her stepmother kicked her out after discovering marijuana in her bedroom. The sixteen-year-old moved in with her twenty-three-year-old boyfriend Rob Beaudry, who was a jumpmaster at the skydiving club that Dana joined.

Dana grew into an athletic, blonde-haired, blue-eyed teenager. She attended Newport Harbor High School, where her classmates were actors Kelly McGillis, Ted McGinley, and motorcycle racer Bruce Penhall, who was the 1981 and 1982 World Speedway Champion. After Dana graduated in 1976, Beaudry helped and encouraged her through nursing school at Saddleback College in Mission Viejo. During this time, Dana twice got pregnant by Rob. Both pregnancies ended by abortion, allegedly at Rob's insistence, but life seemed to be on-track for Dana. Besides parachuting, Dana stayed active in leisure sports and excelled in windsurfing and golf.

Dana graduated from nursing school in 1981, and fulfilled her dream of becoming a nurse. Beaudry was out of her life, but she had an on-again, off-again relationship with fellow windsurfer Chris Dodson, and together they attended windsurfing competitions and golf tournaments all over the west coast. Life appeared good for Dana Sue Armbrust; she had a well-paying hospital job, but she still spent more money that she made.

In 1986, Dana's father married Jeri Davis, a widow. Dana, between jobs and boyfriends, moved in with the couple at their home in Canyon Lake until she could figure out what her next step would be. She was curious about working in Australia or New Zealand. Tom Gray, a fellow sports buff who had admired Dana from afar since high school, also lived in Canyon Lake. He was intrigued when he heard his high school crush lived nearby.

Gray was a drummer in a Southern California rock band named Longshot. They played all the usual L.A. clubs, but none of the band members seemed interested in getting a recording contract or touring outside of Southern

California. Gray piloted ultra-light aircraft and made extra money by towing advertising banners over events in Riverside County, but his day job was operating heavy equipment at construction sites. He earned good money due to the housing boom throughout Riverside County. Dana was smitten with the handsome, long-haired musician, but she had plans to go to Australia and New Zealand to seek new adventures in wind surfing, mountain climbing and other death defying sports. Gray encouraged her adventure and even arranged for a couple of places for her to stay while in Australia.

Tom Gray picked her up at Los Angeles International Airport when she returned. Dana came back from her trip a little dejected. She had found it hard for an American to acquire the proper work permits for employment in Australia. If she did get hired as a nurse, she would be cleaning bedpans for little money. With her experience as a registered nurse, Dana saw it as a slap to her ego to start at the bottom.

In late 1987, Dana took a walk down the aisle and married Tom. She got a taste of better living as the couple bought a home in the exclusive city of Canyon Lake, a small planned city which is entirely gated. The city is patrolled by a private security company, as well as the Riverside County Sheriff's Department. Most houses edge up next to one of the many golf courses, or have docks with access to Canyon Lake. People buy homes there to feel safe, and they pay extra for that peace of mind.

Dana got a job at a small hospital on Catalina Island, where she got to scuba dive every morning before her shift. She came home on her days off. To earn more money, the couple started a wedding service in which Tom, a licensed minister from the Universal Life Church, would marry the couple and the Grays would provide the musical entertainment. Tom had taught Dana how to play the guitar, and like anything that she tried, she excelled at it. They spent thousands of dollars on keyboards, guitars, amplifiers, and recording equipment. The couple also started a silk-screening company, creating custom made T-shirts and banners.

In order to keep up with his active wife, Tom bought the couple bicycles and went on strenuous rides. But Tom could never keep pace with Dana, who put all her power and skill into riding. Like everything that she tried, Dana excelled at it.

Dana, like her mother, lived beyond her means, and it did not take long before the couple had a second mortgage on their home and major credit card debt. They missed house payments. When Tom inherited a couple of thousand dollars from a deceased relative, Dana used the money to visit some friends in Sweden instead of paying off their debts. Dana never missed her hair appointments, weekly manicures and spa dates. Nor did she sell her gold Cadillac.

All bubbles have to burst, and when the housing bubble burst in Southern California at the end of the 1980s, it hit Tom like the heavy machinery he operated. When he could find work, it was only for a limited time. The couple often had loud arguments over her spending and his lack of earning. By this time, Tom learned to just let Dana yell and scream, because yelling back only fed her anger.

Dana started asking her step-brothers and other relatives for money. She angered family members when she tried to change her step-brother's elderly great-aunt's will to include her. As always, Dana exploded in rage at her step-siblings when her motives were questioned. She asked her father to co-sign the refinancing of their Canyon Lake home, but he turned her down because the house was so underwater.

Dana got a job at the nearby Inland Valley Regional Medical Center as a labor and delivery nurse. She took extra shifts at the hospital, which made her even more resentful toward Tom. She threw herself into her silk screening company and her wedding business, but it was like emptying the ocean with a bucket. When Tom cut up a credit card, Dana would just apply for another one.

Then at thirty-three, Dana wanted to have a baby. She hoped it would fix the marriage. In January 1991, Dana became pregnant, but miscarried two months later. Devastated, she became depressed and started drinking. Her doctor put her on Paxil.

With his life in financial ruin, his career in the toilet and an angry wife making his life miserable, Tom rediscovered his love for music, and started a band that rehearsed in his garage. Dana, not wanting to be left out of anything, hung out at rehearsals, where she soon caught the eye of the band's guitarist, Jim Wilkins.

The day before Christmas, 1991, Dana left Tom and moved in with Jim Wilkins and his six-year-old son Jason on Mission Trail in nearby Wildomar. Some thought Dana gave more attention to young Jason than Jim did, as she spent a lot of time nurturing the young boy. During this time, Dana could not make up her mind if she should stay with Wilkins or go back to her husband, so she ping-ponged between the two men for the next year and a half.

Dana finally filed for divorce during the summer of 1993, and in September the couple filed for bankruptcy to protect their biggest asset, their home, from being foreclosed on. Things went from bad to worse when Dana was fired from her job at Inland Valley Regional Medical Center on November 24, 1993, for misappropriating Demerol and other opiates. Dana had already been reprimanded for not getting along with her coworkers, but falsifying narcotic inventory is a serious offense. Dana claimed the missing drugs were either prescribed verbally by doctors or were destroyed when the glass vials fell on the floor. Hospital management did not believe her.

Unbeknownst to Tom Gray, Dana had taken out a life insurance policy on him. On Valentine's Day 1994, Dana tried to have a meet up with Tom. She did not know where he lived or even what his phone number was, but she relayed her request through his parents. Tom did not show up for the rendezvous, a decision that likely saved his life.

After being stood up by her ever-suffering soon-to-be-ex-spouse, Dana drove to Canyon Lake, used her pass key that she never turned in, and gained entrance to the gated town. She drove past her old home, now in foreclosure, and stopped to see eighty-six-year-old Norma Davis, who lived on Continental Drive. Davis was the former mother-in-law of her latest stepmother. Jeri Davis' husband, Bill, died in the early 1980s. Even though she remarried, Dana continued to care for her elderly former mother-in-law. Dana knew Norma from her father and Jeri's family events.

Davis, who was recovering from triple-bypass surgery, let Dana in and then sat back down in her recliner chair. Dana sneaked up behind the elderly woman and strangled her with a phone cord before stabbing her eleven times with two knives. She left a wooden-handled utility kitchen knife in Norma's neck, followed by a fillet knife in the chest. Both knifes were buried to the hilt and she was left nearly decapitated. A concerned neighbor found Norma's body two days later.

Detectives were dumbfounded why anyone would kill such a helpless old woman. With no forced entry, the house barely disturbed, and the victim in her lounging chair, detectives surmised Norma knew her murderer. The only clues police could find were a small shoe print made by a Nike sneaker, a smear of blood on an armchair, and a phone cord that had been ripped out of the wall.

Two weeks later on February 28, 1994, Dana appeared at sixty-six-year-old June Roberts' home on Big Tee Drive in Canyon Lake and asked if she could borrow a book about kicking alcohol addiction. As Roberts led the way to the bookshelf, Gray came up behind her and strangled her with a coiled telephone wire. Gray took cash and two credit cards out of Roberts' purse and quietly left. With barely a hair out of place, Gray went on a shopping spree, using Roberts' credit card to shop at a high-end shopping plaza in Temecula. She then got a massage at the Murrieta Hot Springs Resort.

Thursday, March 10, 1994, was like any other weekday morning at the Main Street Trading Post, an antique store in Lake Elsinore. Dorinda Hawkins, a fifty-seven-year-old mother of eight, was straightening up the store when Dana Sue Gray walked in. Dana looked like any of the well-heeled women who patronized the shop, and Hawkins greeted her in a friendly manner. Gray asked if Hawkins had any antique picture frames. As Hawkins walked Gray to where the frames where, she felt a plastic phone cord wrap around her neck. Gasping and fighting for her life, Gray gently whispered to Hawkins to shhhhh and accept her fate. Leaving her for dead, Gray took five dollars and a credit card out of Hawkins' wallet and twenty dollars out of the store's cash register. Leaving Hawkins lying on the floor, Gray went on a shopping spree.

After lying unconscious on the floor for almost an hour, the telephone rang, waking Hawkins up. She answered the phone and hysterically told the caller what happened and to call the police. She gave an accurate description of her attacker.

Police were confident whoever committed the assault and robbery on Hawkins was connected to the murders of Davis and Roberts, but the big problem was that they had a female serial killer on their hands. The short-staffed Riverside County Sheriff's Department assigned the case to Detective Joseph Greco. Norma Davis was his second homicide case. Greco approached the murders and assault with caution. He needed to assure the citizens of Canyon Lake they were safe, and that the sheriff's department, as well as the private security company the gated city employed, would step up their efforts and catch the killer.

When Dana heard Dorinda Hawkins survived the attack, she got her hair cut short and dyed it red. Unknown to Dana, her father's latest wife,

Jeri Ambrust, was talking with Detective Greco. Jeri told the detective her step-daughter knew Norma Davis, had a key to her home, and still had her access key to Canyon Lake. She resembled the description given by Hawkins, yet detectives did not know Dana had recently changed her appearance. Greco assigned an undercover officer to keep Gray's home, which she shared with her boyfriend and his son on Mission Trail in nearby Wildomar, under surveillance.

March 16, 1994, would be the last day of freedom for Dana Sue Gray. Driving her gold Cadillac, she once again used her access key to pass the gates of Canyon Lake. She slowly drove down the same street Norma Davis had lived on. She watched eighty-seven-year-old Dora Beebe come home from a doctor's appointment, and called out to her. Dana told Beebe she was lost, and needed to look at a map. Although irritated by the request, Beebe let Gray into her home.

Walking behind Beebe, Gray grabbed a phone cord and wrapped it around the older woman's neck. There was a great struggle as furniture was knocked over and glass broke. Gray kept choking the thrashing Beebe until the older woman ran out of strength. Grabbing a nearby clothes iron, Gray hit Beebe in the head until she was dead.

Despite the mess made during the murder, Gray came away surprisingly unscuffed. Rifling through Beebe's purse, she grabbed her wallet, checkbook, and bankbook before leaving. As with the other crimes, Gray went on a shopping spree.

As Gray shopped, Detective Greco received a warrant to search Gray's home, and his team staked-out the place, waiting for her. The police had no idea Gray was returning from another murder. The police sprang into action as Gray pulled her Cadillac, filled with shopping bags, up to her home.

Police found the victims' bankbooks, purses, wallets, and credit cards hidden around the house. Two thousand dollars in cash, the exact amount taken out of June Roberts' bank account, was found in a purse hidden behind the washing machine. The house was filled with brand-new clothes and jewelry, still in their shopping bags.

Police took Gray, Jim Wilkins, and his son Jason to the stationhouse for questioning. They quickly ruled out Wilkins as a suspect or abettor and released him. Gray was charged with murder.

She refused to admit guilt or even talk to the detectives. She caused trouble with other inmates and jail guards separated her from the general population. When detectives visited her in her cell, she would seductively strip off her clothing in front of them. When confronted with the overwhelming evidence she told over-the-top stories and planned to plea insanity.

At her hearing, the prosecution told the court they wanted to ask for the death penalty. Finding out police had witnesses who saw her at Norma Davis' home at the time of the murder, Dana changed her tune. She pleaded guilty to the murders of June Roberts and Dora Beebe, and to the attempted murder of Dorinda Hawkins. She was not charged with the murder of Norma Davis. Her guilty plea saved her from facing the death penalty. The thirty-six-year-old Gray was taken to the California Women's Prison in Chowchilla to serve a life sentence with no chance of parole.

A Mother's Love

October 25 and 27, 1994—324 East Shaver Street, San Jacinto
Murderer: Dora Buenrostro
Victim: Susana, Vicente, and Deidra Buenrostro

On the morning of October 27, 1994, a heavy-set, Hispanic female burst into the Riverside County Sheriff substation in the dusty, working class San Jacinto Valley town of San Jacinto. Thirty-four-year-old Dora Buenrostro screamed at the police that her ex-husband was at her apartment and was going to harm their children. Police rushed to the apartment complex at 324 East Shaver Street and found a scene that made the most veteran deputy throw up. Buenrostro's nine-year-old daughter Susana and eight-year-old son Vicente were dead, their throats slit. Susana was laid out on a loveseat and Vicente on a couch. Both of the children were covered with a blood soaked blanket. Their tiny arms had multiple cuts on them from defending themselves. Four-year-old daughter Deidra was nowhere to be found.

Riverside County sheriffs noticed the lack of emotion Dora displayed when they discovered her children dead, as well as her lack of concern about her missing daughter. She demanded the police arrest her ex-husband, Alex Buenrostro, for the murders. Alex lived in the Los Angeles neighborhood of Silver Lake, so the Los Angeles Police were called to pick him up. The L.A.P.D. found him around two in the morning and took him for a ride to Riverside.

While Alex Buenrostro was in custody, the Riverside County Sheriffs informed him of the death of his two children and the disappearance of another. The news of his children's deaths devastated Alex. Detectives checked with his employer and questioned his friends. They quickly realized Alex Buenrostro not only had an airtight alibi, but he was also utterly distraught over the deaths of his children. Investigators were sure he did not commit the murders. On the other hand, Dora's story changed every time she told it and she was evasive and non-responsive when asked if she knew where her daughter Deidra could be. A Riverside County sheriff's deputy described Dora's behavior: "She went from laughing and joking to being tired to being nonchalant, but never showed remorse or sadness...."

Later that evening, some children playing in an abandoned post office sorting facility at Date Street and Reservoir Avenue in Lakeview found the lifeless body of Deidra. She was strapped in a child seat, and like her siblings, her throat was slit. She appeared to have been dead for several days. The blade of the knife that killed her had broken off in her neck.

Police arrested Dora two days later and charged her with three counts of first degree murder. In July 1998, four years after the murders, she was brought to trial. The jury listened for three weeks as Deputy District Attorney Michael Soccio described the crimes in intense detail. The jury saw crime scene photos of the dead children with their throats slit, and looked at autopsy photos of the children's various wounds. DNA tests confirmed that blood found on Dora's car, purse, and wallet belonged to Deidra. Detectives testified to what they saw at the scene, and the distinct and different reactions the parents had when told their children were dead.

Soccio laid out what happened, starting with the night of October 25th, when Dora visited her ex-husband at his Silver Lake apartment. On her way to see Alex, Dora, who had little Deidra with her, first took her anger out on the four-year-old. She stabbed the girl so violently that the knife blade broke off in her throat, and then Dora coldly left her in a massive abandoned postal facility for the rats to eat. She continued her drive to Silver Lake to see Alex. After they had sex, Dora pulled a knife on Alex and he called the police. Angered at her ex-husband for seeing other women while her own love life was stifled by her three young children, she murdered nine-year-old Susana and eight-year-old Vicente as they lounged in their living room the next day. She spent the rest of the day in her apartment with her two dead children as her audience, rehearsing what she would tell the police.

Just as the jury was on the edge of being overwhelmed by the vileness of this crime, Alex Buenrostro took the stand. He tearfully told what happened the night Deidra was murdered. He described how he was brought in by the police and the emotional impact of learning about the horrible crimes.

Jay Grossman, Dora's attorney, tried his best to paint the entire crime as unplanned, and that Dora's plot was pathetic. He asked to find her guilty of second degree murder. The jury did not buy it. On July 23, 1998, they found Dora Buenrostro guilty of three counts of first degree murder.

The following Monday, the trial went into the penalty phase. Dora took the stand and denied killing the children. She insisted she was being framed, that Alex had murdered her family, and that the Riverside County Sheriff's Department were in on the cover-up. She went on to berate the prosecution and her own defense attorney.

A Spanish interpreter was brought in for Dora when the jury announced that it had agreed on a penalty. As the interpreter translated the verdict, Dora leaned her head forward and cried. She was officially sentenced to death on October 2, 1998. As of this date, she is awaiting execution. Jury members told reporters that had she admitted her guilt and said that she was sorry, they would have given her life without parole.

I Remember Mama

April 4, 1940—1211 West 58th Place, Los Angeles
Murderers: Lolita and Chloe Davis
Victims: Daphne, Deborah, Mark, and Lolita Davis

Eleven-year-old Chloe Davis, woke to a commotion on April 4, 1940. As she stepped out of her bedroom and into the hallway of her home at 1211 West 58th Place in South Los Angeles she was struck across the head with a heavy object. Looking up, she saw her crazed and bloodied mother, Lolita Davis, swinging a hammer. Chloe wrestled the hammer away, but then Lolita tried to light Chloe's hair on fire. When that did not work, she lit her own hair and nightgown on fire.

Lolita asked Chloe to help her move a mattress into the hallway and then told her she had killed Chloe's siblings, ten-year-old Daphne, seven-year-old Deborah, and three-year-old Mark. She murdered them to save them from demons.

Lolita was born Lolita Dell Bjorkman in 1903 and was raised in Grand Rapids, Michigan. In 1926, she married fellow Grand Rapids resident, Barton Davis, and the couple lived in St. Joseph, South Haven and Grand Rapids before moving to Los Angeles in 1938. Barton worked as a supermarket manager, while Lolita kept house and raised their four children. By all accounts, Lolita was a good mother who maintained an immaculate home and kept up on current child-raising practices. She had never shown any signs of mental illness.

Lolita asked Chloe to kill her with a hammer. Chloe hit her mother in the chest with the hammer, but it was not hard enough for Lolita. She lay down on the mattress and told Chloe to beat her harder. Chloe beat her for so long that she had to stop and catch her breath, even getting a glass of water. When little Mark let out a death moan in the kitchen, where Lolita had left him for dead, Lolita told Chloe to put him out of his misery, and Chloe hit him three times in the head with her hammer. Finally Lolita asked Chloe to get her some razor blades out of the bathroom. The dutiful little blonde did as told, and soon Lolita died of blood loss.

Chloe washed up and got dressed before she ran out of the house to call her father at work. Barton found his wife and son dead. Daughters Daphne

and Deborah would be dead on arrival to the hospital. Barton wailed in grief while Chloe stood as calm as if she waited for a bus. She allegedly told him to calm down.

The baffled police took Chloe to headquarters to question her more thoroughly. Chloe told her story unemotionally. Police were suspicious of her account. It was too calculated, and she was too calm for having witnessed the deaths of her mother and siblings. They thought she alone had murdered her family, but when the autopsies came back and Lolita was found to have died from blood loss, they realized Chloe had told the truth. Her stoic behavior came from the emotional and mental shock of the ordeal. She had finished off her little brother with three hammer blows to the head, but she was only obeying her mother.

Authorities released Chloe to Barton, and the two of them left Los Angeles, eventually settling in the Midwest.

He Who Laughs Last

May 28, 1998—5065 Encino Avenue, Encino
Murderer: Brynn Hartman
Victim: Phil Hartman

Every day, dozens of young actors, actresses, comedians, and musicians arrive in Los Angeles eager for their big chance to make it in show business. There is no way to know how many of them achieve their goal, but it cannot be a high percentage. Many end up working on the technical or business end of the industry. Others wind up in an entirely different career in the City of Angels. A lot decide to leave Los Angeles and go home, dejected and angry at the city that promised them nothing.

Then there are those who cling onto the edges of showbiz. Those whose career is one of bit parts on almost cancelled television programs or a session gig for scale on a hit song. Missed opportunities, bad decisions, clueless agents . . . the list is endless. Few things are worse for an actor than getting passed over for parts time and time again. Seeing old roommates, coworkers, or lovers find Hollywood success for no apparent reason other than pure dumb luck, or for performing sexual favors to advance their career. Los Angeles has more secrets than any other city on Earth.

Vicki Jo Omdahl was one of those hopeful actors. She left her home in Thief River Falls, Minnesota, after a failed marriage. She had done some modeling in Minneapolis, and around 1978 moved to Los Angeles to take acting lessons and advance her career in modeling. She changed her name. She first went with Vicki, then Vicki Jo, then Brindon and finally Brynn.

The film and television roles always went to some other beautiful statuesque blonde, and to deaden the rejection, or merely for the fun of it, Omdahl turned to cocaine and alcohol. By 1985, Brynn got sober and made a living as a swimsuit model. In 1986, she met actor/comedian Phil Hartman at a Hollywood party. Hartman had recently finalized his divorce from his second wife, Lisa Strain, and friends said he was in a vulnerable state. Hartman had a pattern of falling in love quickly—and hard—so it came as no surprise when he and Brynn began an intense relationship.

Phil Hartman, born Phillip Edward Hartmann on September 24, 1948, in Brantford, Ontario, was the middle child of a large Catholic family. At

ten, Phil and his family immigrated to the United States. In order to get attention in his large family, Phil did imitations of movies stars and told jokes he had heard on television. He learned at a young age to stay out of trouble and to avoid drama, a trait that would not work out well for him in the long run.

By the time he met Brynn, Hartman had become a successful graphic designer who had designed the Crosby, Stills, and Nash logo, and multiple album covers for the Fireside Theater, Poco, and America. He had been in the legendary improvisational comedy group The Groundlings for nine years, owned his own home, and did voice-over and commercial work on local Los Angeles radio and television. He had co-written *Pee Wee's Big Adventure*, a film in which he also had a role, and had acted in the films ¡*Three Amigos!* and *Jumpin' Jack Flash*.

Hartman's closest friends grew concerned over his and Brynn's quickly progressing love affair and feared Hartman would blindly jump into a another volatile relationship. His star had begun to rise when he and Brynn started their relationship; *Saturday Night Live* had just hired him to join the cast in New York City.

Hartman was credited for bringing *SNL* back from the brink of cancelation. The smooth-talking Hartman had impeccable comic timing and his impressions of Phil Donahue, Barbara Bush, Frank Sinatra, Ronald Reagan, Charlton Heston, Bill Clinton, and Ed McMahon were the glue that held the cast together (which at that time included Jan Hooks, Jon Lovitz, Victoria Jackson, Dana Carvey, and Kevin Nealon). Being older than the rest of the cast, he had a calming effect on the others. Moving to New York City completely disrupted Brynn's life, however. The heavy workload and stress that came with working at *SNL* meant less time for their relationship, yet it did not stop them from tying the knot on November 25, 1987.

Seven months later, Brynn gave birth to Sean Edward. Phil's second wife, Lisa, sent a congratulations card with a personal message to the child from her. Always insecure and jealous, Brynn wrote a malicious four-page letter threatening Lisa if she ever came near her child or Phil.

In February 1992, Brynn gave birth to their second child, Birgen Akika. By all accounts Brynn was an excellent mother, but due to her frustration with being the wife of a famous comedic actor, and knowing her chances of personal stardom were pretty much over, she often lashed out at Phil in front of their friends. A natural beauty, Brynn became obsessed with her body image, undergoing several plastic surgery procedures. She exercised almost daily, keeping her body fit and toned in case Hollywood called her with a part.

By 1994, Hartman had grown tired of the grind of being on a weekly live television program and all of its demands. The original group who came aboard with him had left the show, and he found himself as the old man on the program. After having worked on *SNL* for eight years, and performing in one hundred fifty-three shows, Hartman left *SNL* and moved his family back to Los Angeles.

Hartman acted in a handful of comedic films during his time in New York City, and most of them, like *So I Married an Axe Murderer, Sgt. Bilko,* and *CB4,* were not exactly box office smashes. Hartman did several voices on *The Simpsons* since 1991, including slimy attorney Lionel Hutz and faded action actor Troy McClure. His characters appeared on over fifty-two episodes of the iconic cartoon series.

In 1995, Hartman signed on to a new television program called *News Radio* on NBC. Hartman played Bill McNeal, an arrogant New York City radio newsman. The cast included former *Kids in the Hall* alumnus Dave Foley, award-winning actress Khandi Alexander, future *ER* actress Maura Tieney, and comedians Stephen Root, Joe Rogan, and Andy Dick. A young Vicki Lewis played Beth, the ditsy secretary. Although the show was an ensemble, never focusing on one character for too long, the network paid Hartman a whopping fifty thousand dollars an episode. Although *News Radio* was not a hit show, it managed to stay on NBC's schedule for four years.

Acting work all but avoided Brynn. In 1994, she had a tiny speaking role as "waitress" in the Rob Reiner flop *North,* a film most known for the incredibly negative review the late film critic Roger Ebert wrote. Four years later, Brynn picked up a small role as a Venusian in a two-part episode of the NBC comedy *Third Rock from the Sun.* Her career was as sunk as the *Titanic.*

Falling deep into depression, Brynn fell off the wagon and started drinking and doing cocaine. Her doctor prescribed Zoloft, which only clouded Brynn's delicate mind. At home, the couple argued incessantly, and bickered when out with friends, which embarrassed Phil tremendously. Phil's way of dealing with their problems was to buy another toy to have fun with.

Hartman rented an airplane hangar at the Van Nuys Airport where he stored his airplane, motorcycles, and automobile collection. He also owned a Boston Whaler boat that he would use to cruise out to the Catalina Islands, twenty-five-miles off Los Angeles, every chance he could. His hobbies made Brynn suspicious, and she went as far as hiring a private detective to see what he was doing away from home. She convinced herself he was romantically involved with another woman, or man. The homophobic Brynn feared that her husband may be having an affair with one of his close friends. The detective came up with zilch. Phil responded to Brynn's mental and chemical problems by not speaking to her.

May 27, 1998, appeared to be just another day in the dysfunctional life at the Hartman home. Phil came home around 6 p.m. after spending the afternoon with a buddy of his. They had hung out together shopping for supplies for their Boston Whaler boats. Brynn had made plans to meet with a girlfriend of hers, Christine Zander, at Buca di Beppo, a nearby restaurant.

Brynn bent her friend's ear complaining about her marriage and career while downing two Cosmopolitans and a beer chaser. Despite Brynn's criticism of her husband, she told Zander they were actually getting along better than ever. During the two hours the friends were together, Brynn went suspiciously to the restroom twice. Zander called it a night around 9:30 p.m. Brynn drove to Studio City to see a longtime acquaintance, Ron Douglas, at his home. Douglas was a former lover of Brynn's from their hard partying days in the 1980s. Douglas quit the party scene years before and worked as a stuntman.

To Douglas, Brynn did not appear to be drunk, even though she drank three cans of beer in quick succession. Douglas let Brynn talk in between the half-dozen phone calls she made while there. It was the same old things that she complained about: her career and her husband. Douglas finally got Brynn to go home around 12:45 a.m.

Brynn arrived home at 5065 Encino Boulevard around one in the morning, and from this point no one knows what happened between her and Phil. They could have argued about Brynn's relapse into chemical dependency until Phil did what he often did while they were endlessly fighting—he went to sleep.

Brynn took a Smith & Wesson .38 caliber pistol, one of the many firearms in the Hartman home, walked over to their bed, and fired three shots into her sleeping husband. One shot entered the right side of Phil's neck. The next went through his arm and into his chest. Both of those shots were fired from less than eighteen inches away. The third shot, fired point-blank between the eyes, blew Hartman's brains out. It is unclear in what order the shots were fired.

Brynn drove back to Douglas' house and babbled incoherently about what she had done. He followed her back to her house, went inside, and found Phil's bloody body. Phil had a grin on his face. Douglas called 911.

Police showed up to find Brynn locked in her bedroom with Phil's body. They herded the children out of the house and planned on breaking into the barricaded bedroom through a window, but Brynn put a bullet through her head before they could act. The Hartman children grew up as orphans.

The Doctor's Wife, Part III

November 22, 1999— 12000 Presilla Road, Camarillo
Murderer: Socorro "Cora" Caro
Victim: Xavier Jr., Michael, and Christopher Caro

The homes along the 12000 block of Presilla Road would be impressive anywhere. Tastefully ornate iron gates guard the long asphalt driveways leading to spectacularly large homes that cling to the side of the Santa Rosa Valley in Camarillo, California. Doctor Xavier Caro, a renowned expert in rheumatology with a successful practice in nearby Northridge, lived in his five-bedroom, four-bathroom mansion on eight acres with his wife Socorro, who was known to everyone as Cora. They lived there with their children, eleven-year-old Xavier Jr., eight-year-old Michael, five-year-old Christopher, and Gabriel, their one-year-old. The University of California, Los Angeles, graduate bought the home in 1993 and it was said to be worth over five-million dollars in 2000. Xavier and Cora married in 1986 and enjoyed the success that enabled them to live in luxury.

Cora worked as the office manager at Dr. Caro's medical complex for fifteen years, but in 1998 Cora got sticky fingers. She began siphoning money from the business and giving it to her parents, Greg and Juanita Leon. The Leons, who lived in nearby Granada Hills, were a fixture at the house on Presilla Road, and even had their own room at the estate. The couple acted the role of grandparents, with Juanita watching the kids and Greg, a retired bricklayer, puttering around the compound.

When the doctor discovered his wife had embezzled over a hundred thousand dollars from his practice, he fired her from her position, just as he would any employee. She no longer had access to the company's funds. It is not like she needed the job. Needless to say, the marriage was wobbly, and that was compounded by Cora's alcohol consumption and a brief affair the handsome doctor had with a colleague. The two worked on their relationship and seemed to be doing much better.

On November 22, 1999, the Caro family had a light dinner and settled in for a quiet evening at home. Xavier Jr., now twelve, made a sarcastic comment about his parents having an extra Margarita, which angered the doctor. Anyone who has ever been around preteen children knows that

there are few stages of life that are so difficult for both the child and everyone else within a thirty-foot radius. For punishment, Xavier took away his son's computer games, which angered Cora, and the couple started bickering. Xavier decided it would be more constructive to head over to his practice to catch up on paperwork, and let Cora cool down.

While at the office, Cora telephoned him three different times, crying so hysterically he could not understand her. He told her he would be home shortly. He left his office around 10:30 p.m., the surveillance cameras at his building's parking lot dutifully recording his departure in his Mercedes-Benz. When he arrived at his spectacular home he found Cora on the floor of their bedroom. He called police and while talking to the dispatcher discovered a bullet wound on the right side of Cora's head, and her .38 caliber revolver underneath her body. Panicking, he ran to his son's bedrooms, only to find Xavier Jr. and Michael in their beds, both shot once in the head. Five-year-old Christopher must have woken up when he heard the gunshots, as it took two bullets to the head to kill him. Cartoon sheets and superhero-themed pillows were soaked in blood and brain tissue. Xavier got back on the telephone to the emergency dispatcher and mournfully cried that his children were all shot, except for the infant Gabriel. For some reason, Cora did not have the nerve to kill her baby.

Cora's attempt at suicide was bungled. The bullet did not pierce her skull; it instead zipped around under her scalp, leaving her bloody but not seriously injured. A blood test revealed Cora had twice the legal amount of alcohol to be considered intoxicated in the state of California. Also in her blood was Prozac, an anti-depressant prescribed to her. Police arrested Cora and charged her with three counts of first degree murder.

The four-month-long trial started on August 23, 2001, in Ventura County Superior Court, almost twenty months after the murders. Cora's defense was completely implausible. Her attorneys originally tried to place the murders on the doctor, a theory easily destroyed by Deputy District Attorney Jim Ellison, who established a timeline with phone records and surveillance photos from the doctor's office and parking garage. Xavier's hands and clothing had no trace of gunpowder. The prosecution also provided witnesses who described seeing Cora's violent side on multiple occasions, once giving her husband a black eye. Another witness told the court on one occasion Cora told her she wanted to commit suicide.

Socorro took the stand and blamed Xavier for the murders and that he was framing her for the crimes. Cora cried during her testimony, and twice was removed by the court because of her sobbing. After twenty-four minutes of testimony, Cora was dismissed from the witness chair. Her attorney's changed her plea to "Innocent by Reason of Insanity."

The jurors deliberated for five days before reaching a guilty verdict. A judge later sentenced her to death for her crimes and she is currently sitting on death row in San Quentin State Prison.

Doctor Xavier Caro and his surviving son, Gabriel, moved to a new house where they have attempted to return to as much of a normal life as they possibly could.

What's a Girl to Do?

January 6, 1953—978 Piedmont Drive, Sacramento
Murderer: Jeanette Rohr
Victim: Fern Carson

No one will ever really know the exact relationship fifty-one-year-old Fern Carson had with thirty-four-year-old Jeanette Alyse Rohr. Fern and her husband, Bradford, had taken in Jeanette to live with them after Jeanette's mother had been committed to a mental hospital in 1938. The Carsons were kind to Jeanette, making sure she got an education and a useful skill so she could earn a livelihood. Working as a dental hygienist, Rohr made a good living for a single woman in the 1950s, but for some reason Rohr never moved out on her own She stayed with her adopted family in an idyllic Sacramento neighborhood well into her middle age.

Jeanette told Fern she planned to marry Polk Overholt, a young man from Folsom she had dated over the holidays. At first Fern thought she was joking, but Jeanette insisted she was serious. Somehow it all came to a head on January 6, 1953.

Coming home at 3 p.m. from his job as a clerk for the railroad, Bradford found Fern naked on their blood-soaked bed. Her face was bashed in by a heavy object, and she had multiple stab wounds on her chest made by a barbecue fork protruding from her stomach. She was covered in dried blood and long dead. Calling out for Jeanette, he heard her moaning in the bathroom. He found her in a hysterical state, sitting in a bathtub of bloody water and clad only in her underwear.

Ambulances and police rushed to the home. Jeanette was taken to a hospital and the coroner was called for Fern. The crime scene baffled the Sacramento police. Investigators were faced with a magnitude of questions to answer, such as why was Fern naked in her bed during the day? And why did the killer use a barbecue fork, a very unconventional weapon? Because there were no signs of a struggle, the police wanted to know if Fern was asleep before being beaten with a wrench, or if she trusted the person with her. Then investigators had to explain how Jeanette ended up in the bathtub, nearly naked, and suffering from stab wounds.

After getting stitched up, Rohr told police what happened that cold Tuesday morning. According to Jeanette, the women were hanging around the house and Jeanette once again brought up her desire to marry Polk. Mrs. Carson, tired of hearing such nonsense, angrily told Rohr she forbade her to marry him. Rohr went outside to the tool shed and picked up a large, heavy pipe wrench. She walked back into the house and into the Carson's bedroom. Fern Carson was lying naked and uncovered on her bed. Jeanette walked up to her and clubbed her several times in the head.

The younger woman then went to the kitchen, grabbed a three prong barbecue fork, and stabbed the already dead woman multiple times. Covered in blood, Rohr went outside, took off her blood covered clothes, and dove into the Carson's swimming pool in an attempt to drown herself. A neighbor from across the street saw Rohr in the backyard and heard the splashing of the water in the pool. She found it odd Jeanette would be taking a dip in the pool on such a chilly day.

Intentionally drowning oneself is not as easy as it sounds, so when Rohr realized she could not go through with it, she ran back into the house, half-dressed, and took a knife from the kitchen. She went into the bath-room, filled the bathtub, and got in. She first tried to electrocute herself by dropping an electric radio into the bath, but it just harmlessly blew out a fuse. Finally, Jeanette began stabbing herself while she doubled over in the water-filled tub.

Police later found out Rohr was being treated for a nervous disorder. When police interviewed Polk Overholt, he told them he had only gone on four casual dates with Rohr and barely knew her, as they spent most of their dates going to see movies, and then out dancing with their friends.

Why did Fern Carson have so much influence over Jeanette's romantic life? Why where both women found naked or near naked? Were the two lovers?

We will likely never know. Jeanette Rohr was committed to a mental hospital and dropped out of history not long afterward.

The Grifter

September 10, 2001—Lodi, San Joaquin County
Murderer: Elisa McNabney
Victim: Larry McNabney

Grifters fascinate us. There is something enthralling and exhilarating about using deception and charm to cheat someone out of their money. The smart grifters have their own cults or religions, but the best grifters are the ones you never hear about. Laren Sims had promise, but she screwed up when her partying lifestyle caught up with her.

Born to an upper-middle class family, Laren Sims grew up Brooksville, Florida. Once in her teens, she started hanging out with the wrong crowd, and like the old cliché, it led to nothing but trouble. By 1986, she had been married twice and had two children, but motherhood did not stop her compulsive criminal behavior. She agreed to let her second husband have custody of their son and Sims traveled with her daughter, Haylei Jordan, using her name as one of her many aliases. Sims allegedly had over thirty aliases; among the known ones were Elisa Redelsperger, Shane Ivaroni, Tammy Lynn Keelin, Melissa Wynell Goodwin, and Loren Jordan. As a grifter Laren must have had her share of successes, because she had her share of getting caught too. At first her parents paid for attorneys, but eventually took up the then current sociological trend of tough love. By 1993, Sims had racked up a rap sheet that went on for over a hundred pages, detailing acts of burglary, forgery, credit card fraud, grand theft, and violation of parole. While serving prison time she met Elizabeth "Elisa" Barasch, and took her name when she cut off her ankle monitor and went on the lam with her daughter. They ended up in Las Vegas where Laren Sims, using the name Elizabeth Barasch, married thirty-five-year-old businessman Kenneth Redelsperger.

In 1995, Elizabeth Redelsperger walked into the law firm of Larry McNabney and applied for a job. By 1996, Laren, a.k.a. Elizabeth Redelsperger, became Elizabeth "Elisa" McNabney, the fifth wife of Larry McNabney.

Larry McNabney came from pioneer Reno, Nevada, stock. His grandfather, Guy McNabney, was an early city booster and his father, James, who

went by "Mac," carried on the family tradition of civil service. Mac married Marie Williams in 1943, just as he left for military service during World War II. Marie came from a financially connected family as her father was the superintendent of a gold mine. After the war, Mac and Marie settled down to raise a family. James Junior was born in 1947, and Laurence "Larry" Williams McNabney was born in 1948.

When the Korean War broke out in June 1950, Mac got recalled to the military. There are no records indicating what Mac did while on duty in that conflict, but he came home with post-traumatic stress disorder. Mac managed the campus bookstore of the University of Nevada-Reno, and owned a nice house for his family to live in. He was stern with his sons and demanded they succeed in academic and athletic pursuits. James and Larry excelled at both. Mac spent his time self-medicating with alcohol. In 1968, a daughter, Cristin, was born to the couple.

Larry met a girl in his last year of high school; he got her pregnant and the two married. Larry attended the University of Nevada-Reno and graduated in 1970. He and his young family moved to Sacramento so he could attend the McGeorge School of Law, which is affiliated with the University of the Pacific in Stockton. She hated living so far away from her family in Reno and soon left Larry and moved back to Reno. During this time of stress, Larry dropped out of law school and became obligated to fulfill his contract with the Reserve Officers Training Corps (ROTC), which had helped him attend college with the stickler he serve in the military after he graduated from college.

With her sons grown and in the military (James was in the Navy), Marie decided she had enough of Mac's abuse and filed for divorce. The couple had made some wise investments, including stocks in Pacific Telephone and Telegraph, Sierra Pacific, Northwest Bell, and AT&T. They also owned a large home on Brown Street in Reno. Instead of answering the divorce complaint, Mac shot himself. Three weeks later, Larry's older brother James took an intentional drug overdose.

Larry married again in 1973, and the next year graduated from McGeorge and was appointed clerk at the Reno District Court. He took and passed the bar exams for both Nevada and California and joined the Washoe County Public Defender's Office in the juvenile department. By 1977, Larry left the public defender's office and started a firm with another attorney from Reno, Ron Bath.

The firm handled criminal cases, drugs related crimes, gamblers who ran into trouble with one of the many Reno casinos, and murderers. The firm made a ton of money, and based themselves in a remodeled mansion near the courthouse. Larry averaged five murder cases each year. Instead of pleading a deal with the prosecutor, Larry would take the case to a jury trial. He also won some big liability cases against deep pocketed insurance companies.

Larry became the biggest and brightest attorney in Reno, which not only made him rich, but also earned the admiration of his peers. Yet he was restless. Always a heavy drinker, Larry also smoked marijuana and snorted cocaine. Like in any occupation, drug abuse by attorneys was not a rarity in the 1970s, and Larry would go on binges and became less reliable.

Larry's success was the envy of any attorney, but eventually the stress of his failed marriages, the drugs and his daily contact with Reno lowlifes took its toll. In the summer of 1988, Larry walked away from his practice and moved with his new girlfriend to rural Yelm, Washington, on the southern shore of the Puget Sound.

Larry took up carpentry and enjoyed the work. He earned some money doing finishing work on cabinets for a local builder. It was a happy time for McNabney in the lush Pacific Northwest, making something with his hands. He dabbled in Ramtha's School of Enlightenment, led by JZ Knight, who channeled a 35,000-year-old enlightened spirit named Ramtha, but as with everything else he did, Larry lost interest after a short time studying it. It took less than two years for Larry to miss the legal business, and he jumped back into the jungle of law. Like everything Larry did, he went headfirst.

Moving back to Reno, Larry opened Larry McNabney & Associates, a law firm that specialized in personal injury lawsuits. The plan was to create professional television commercials for the firm, with Larry as the well-dressed, no BS, trustful star, and plaster the ads on every television station in Nevada. The ads were a hit and in 1995 Larry opened two more offices, one in Elko, the other in Las Vegas.

Larry McNabney & Associates made money by volume. The firm collected between 25 to 40 percent of the gross settlement. To handle such volume the firm farmed out cases to other attorneys. Malpractice, accidents, negligence, pain and suffering added up to hundreds of thousands of dollars filling up McNabney's bank accounts. The firm leased a private jet for the many trips between Reno and Las Vegas.

In Vegas, Larry became a minor celebrity and people recognized him in public as that guy in those commercials. He loved the attention, and was soon living it up as the private jet owning, high-rolling attorney with the luxury apartment in Las Vegas and money falling out of his pocket. True to form, however, Larry fell hard off the wagon. Alcohol and drugs crept back into his life. He never got on that wagon again.

By 1995, Elizabeth Redelsperger had divorced her husband Kenneth, and in early summer walked into Larry McNabney & Associates plush Las Vegas office to apply for the office manager position. Larry was captivated with the charming and attractive Elisa, and hired her on the spot. They shared personality traits like reckless, drug-induced behavior, spending money and showing off. Within days Elisa moved into McNabney's luxury condo.

Putting someone like Laren Sims in charge of a multi-million dollar business was akin to a brewery hiring alcoholics to drive their trucks. Nothing good could come out of it. To Laren, now Elisa, it was her dream come true. She had access to the firm's money, checks and credit cards. The days of small scale scams were over. Laren had bagged a rich attorney who spent most of his waking hours wasted on drugs and booze. When the firm's Las Vegas bookkeeper left, Elisa took over. With that position came McNabney's rubber stamp signature, and Elisa was free to write her own checks. The money to the firm poured out as fast as it came in. The couple had matching Jaguar cars, took first-class trips to expensive places, and bought a mountain of pricey clothing and accessories. Larry was rarely in the office, preferring to spend his time snorting coke, smoking powerful marijuana and drinking until he passed out. He went on binges where no one knew his whereabouts for days at a time. It suited Elisa fine.

When Larry found out about the missing checks, which were already bouncing, he sobered up long enough to secure loans from friends and business associates to make things right. The Nevada Bar would be certain to get involved and there would be hell to pay. The associates at the firm begged Larry to fire Elisa, but he shocked everyone by marrying her instead on January 6, 1996.

Larry's friends and associates figured the couple had incriminating dirt on one other, and as in the Cold War between the United States and the

Soviet Union, it would be mutually assured destruction if one betrayed the other.

In March 1997, the Nevada State Bar Association found Larry McNabney guilty of unprofessional conduct, improperly permitting his clients' trust funds to be misused, and failing to properly supervise employees. Elisa was banned from working at Nevada law firms. McNabney managed to get the Bar to modify the reprimands, but Reno is the biggest little town in America, so everyone in Reno's close-knit law community knew what had occurred. The ordeal embarrassed McNabney and he stayed away from his lifelong friends and colleagues. He started selling his homes and property. He and Elisa moved into increasingly lower quality apartments. His grown sons only occasionally heard from him.

In late 1998, the McNabneys decided to get a fresh start in Sacramento. It is an easy move, only a little over a hundred miles from Reno. Being the capital of California, which varies between being the fifth and twelfth largest economy in the world, an abundance of legal work can be found, and, best of all, Elisa was not banned from working at a law office in California. Larry got an office near California State University-Sacramento and had his Nevada commercials edited for California, with his new phone number and address. The ads started airing in early 1999, and in appearance, the couple seemed to be on their way back to the top.

Instead of being in the office, Larry spent time drinking and playing golf. The firm only had to answer phone calls and deal with insurance companies, tasks which Elisa excelled at. Larry only had to go to the office to sign complaints and authorize settlements. They hired a staff, and among them was a twenty-year-old CSUS art student, Sarah Dutra, who has gone down as the biggest, most naïve dupe in the history of California.

Elisa, who was twelve years older than Dutra, took an immediate shining to the Vacaville native and took her on as her personal assistant. Growing up in a working class town that actually translates to "Cow Town," Dutra could not believe her luck. After finishing classes for the day, she would go to the nearby office and run off on adventures with Elisa. The two would eat in expensive restaurants, go to movies and shop for clothes. Elisa gave her a car, allegedly under Dutra's name, to establish her credit, and took her on trips to Las Vegas, Los Angeles, and exclusive Mexican ocean-side resorts.

Larry had been interested in showing American quarter horses, and on New Years' Day, 2001, bought an eight-month old sorrel colt named Justa

Lotta Page for twelve thousand dollars. By then the McNabneys were living in Woodbridge, forty miles south of Sacramento. Justa Lotta Page was kept at a horse farm outside of Lodi, a dozen miles south of Elk Grove. The halter horse was bred to be shown by leading it through the show ring. Larry enjoyed showing his equestrian trophy at the many horse shows around the west coast. Larry also enjoyed dressing up and leading his horse through its paces in front of a crowd. Larry also delighted in being around people like Greg Whalen and his adult daughter Debbie Kail, who trained and cared for Justa Lotta Page.

Showing quarter horses is an expensive hobby. The boarding and training of Justa Lotta Page put McNabney back two thousand dollars a month. Add in the entrance fees to horse shows, transportation to the events, hotels, food, and clothes, and we are talking about some real money. Having to be the best-dressed and biggest spender, McNabney only bought the best boots, hats, and gear. He also bought a six-wheel diesel pickup truck to haul his custom climate controlled horse trailer, which included a dressing/sleeping room that came in handy when Larry needed to sleep off a binge.

The American Quarter Horse Association circuit took Larry, Elisa, and, much to Larry's grief, Sarah Dutra, to Santa Rosa, Santa Barbara, Rancho Murietta, Bakersfield, Las Vegas, Arizona, and Washington State. These meets would last a week and were filled with cocktail parties and dinners. Larry's entourage included Whalen, Kail, Elisa and Sarah, who ran up his American Express card to eighty grand.

With Larry was tramping around Whalen's horse farm or running around quarter horse events, Elisa was robbing Larry McNabney & Associates blind. Clients, attorneys, bills and rent were not being paid while Elisa lived the high life with Sarah. Laren Sims, the lifelong grifter from Florida, had finally hit the jackpot. After a spending her entire adult life with small cons, she now had what seemed as an endless supply of cash, a drunken and easily bullied husband. And if things turned out poorly, she could make the naïve Sarah Dutra take the fall.

By the summer of 2001, creditors and angry clients made up most of the telephone calls to the firm. Extra employees were hired just to ward off calls to Elisa. The scam had neared the tipping point, but Elisa's grifter sense of survival was dulled by the massive amount of alcohol and marijuana she and Sarah consumed. There was too much money and too much fun to be had to think of what would happen when it came crashing down. Elisa had drained all the firm's accounts, several trusts set up for clients, as well as Larry's personal bank accounts.

While at a quarter horse show at the City of Industry, a city made up almost entirely of industrial and commercial zones twenty-two miles east of Los Angeles, Larry showed signs of stress. He felt too ill to show Justa Lotta Page and hid in his hotel room. Elisa and Sarah hobnobbed with their fellow horse people during the day and went out to clubs at night.

On September 10, 2001, Elisa and Sarah spiked Larry's wine with Acepromazine, a powerful horse tranquilizer, and let the effects take its course. Elisa injected the drug through the cork so Larry was none the wiser. They enjoyed the festivities of the horse show and the nightlife of Los Angeles, while Larry slowly succumbed to an overdose of horse tranquilizer.

When they came stumbling back to the hotel room in the early morning hours of September 11, Larry was still alive. He could not move and managed to only mumble incoherent words. Elisa and Sarah put him in a wheelchair and pushed him through the hotel lobby to the parking garage where they loaded him into the back cab of Larry's truck.

Elisa drove to the barns to tell Whalen that Larry had run off to join a cult in Florida and left all of his stuff, which she immediately started to give away. When asked how Larry left, Elisa told them he flew. Whalen, like everyone on September 11, was upset over the World Trade Center attacks earlier that morning, and found it strange that Elisa acted indifferently about the news. Debbie Kail told Elisa that every flight in the United States was grounded because of the attacks. Elisa insisted Larry boarded a flight before the attacks. Whalen, used to working for eccentric rich people, shrugged it off. He had seen Larry's erratic behavior before and knew it would eventually work out. He did think it was odd seeing a folded wheelchair, two new shovels and articles of clothing tossed about in the cab.

Elisa and Sarah took the longest and most difficult route possible back to Lodi. They first headed east into the desert, then up Highway 395, which parallels the rugged eastern side of the Sierra Nevada Mountains. The trio drove past Owens Lake and the towns of Lone Pine and Bishop, finally turning west on Highway 120 at Lee Vining. Larry was still alive when they entered Yosemite National Park and drove the beautiful Tioga Road and down the hairpin curves of Big Oak Flat Road, finally reaching the house in Woodbridge, hours after they would have arrived had they taken Interstate

5. Larry eventually died, and the women put him in a refrigerator in the garage until they could figure out a plan. Elisa and Sarah went on with their party girl ways until Larry's friends and family started getting too nosy about the whereabouts of Larry.

As a Missing Person report was filed, the law firm fell behind in rent, and clients and attorneys were not getting paid. Elisa decided things were getting too hot with Larry in the refrigerator, so with Sarah's help they put him in the trunk of her Jaguar and drove to Las Vegas, where there are plenty of places to dispose of bodies. They got a good startle when at the Bellagio Hotel a security guard asked Sarah to pop the Jaguar's trunk, to which Elisa hopped out, closed the lid and drove off to another hotel. For two days the pair scouted the desert surrounding Las Vegas, seeking a good burial spot for Larry. They found the hard-baked desert earth too hard to dig, so they eventually buried Larry one night during a pouring rain in a vineyard a dozen or so miles from their home.

On February 5, 2002, vineyard workers discovered Larry's leg sticking out of a shallow grave. Elisa McNabney went on the run with her seventeen-year-old daughter Haylei in tow. Both the San Joaquin and the Sacramento County Sheriff Departments were on the case, and since they did not know who Elisa McNabney really was, police turned to Sarah Dutra, who was still living in the same apartment and still drove the same car. Dutra acted as if she had no clue that they had done anything wrong. Either she was playing dumb to the authorities or she was not very intelligent.

In the meantime, Elisa dyed her hair and lost thirty pounds. She and Haylei traveled in the Jaguar toward Florida, pulling small cons along the way for gas and hotel money. Finally, knowing the authorities were moving in on her whereabouts, Elisa sat down on the sand at Fort Walton Beach, Florida, and smoked all of the marijuana she had on her. Okaloosa County sheriff deputies arrested her just after 10:15 p.m. on March 18. The next day, Elisa McNabney reverted back to being Laren Sims and wrote a detailed confession, implementing Sarah Dutra in the murder of Larry McNabney. San Joaquin County sent detectives to Florida to start extradition procedures on Sims. Simultaneously, detectives were sent to Sacramento to pick up the compliant Dutra.

It was inconceivable to Laren Sims that going to prison, possibly for life, was an option. She wrote letters to her children, now both adults, and to her attorney. Ever the scammer, Laren told her attorney to sue the jail she was held in, as it was run by a private corporation and not by the county.

A private company can be sued for more money than a state-owned jail. Sims then ripped her bed sheets into strips, braided them into a rope and hanged herself in her cell.

Sarah Dutra was convicted of manslaughter in San Joaquin County Court and given the maximum penalty under California law—eleven years and eight months in prison. Dutra was released on August 26, 2011, after serving her full term.

Larry McNabney went to his death without ever knowing his fifth wife's real name.

The Acid Queen

July 10, 2003—1602 Houston Avenue, Clovis
Murderer: Larissa Schuster
Victim: Timothy Schuster

Some people believe marriage is a sacrament, while others believe it is a tradition. Once when asked on a television talk show if she thought marriage was an institution, singer/actress Cher replied, "Yes, but who wants to live in an institution?" It would be easy to say that being married to Larissa Schuster could have put anyone into an institution, but being the ex-husband of Larissa Schuster was death.

Larissa Foreman was born in 1960, and grew up as a farm girl outside Clarence, Missouri. She attended the University of Missouri and studied biochemistry. She met Timothy Schuster at a nursing home where they both worked. Schuster was a nursing student from Golden, Illinois, about sixty-miles northeast as the crow flies from Clarence, Missouri. As with most farming communities in the Midwest, both towns are bleak and desolate, sitting in the middle of corn, beets, or soybeans fields as if they were dropped there the way a cow defecates in a field. Foreman and Schuster likely bonded over a shared experience of living in one of the flattest and dullest places in America.

The two dullards got married in 1982, and in 1985 Larissa gave birth to their daughter Kristin. Four years later, Larissa took a job at an agriculture research lab in Fresno, California, so the family packed up and moved from central Missouri to central California. Larissa then gave birth to a son, Tyler, in 1990. Timothy found a job as a nursing administrator at St. Agnes Medical Center and the Schuster family looked as if they were going to settle down into a nice, quiet, middle-class life. They attended Hope Lutheran Church, and Tim joined the Clovis Masonic Lodge.

Larissa noticed warning signs that the lab she worked at was failing. Instead of sinking with the rest of her coworkers, she decided to open and operate her own agriculture research laboratory, Central California Research Labs, at 4672 West Jennifer Avenue. Fresno County is the number one agriculture county in the United States, and the potential of having a

successful ag lab in the Fresno area is a pretty good gamble. Just about everything grows in the Fresno area, as long as the irrigation canals are full.

Central California Research Labs became successful, but running the business put stress on the Schuster's family life. Tim had always been the caretaker of the family, the one who took the children to school, made dinner and tucked Kristin and Tyler in bed at night. Larissa, on the other hand, had to keep up with all the latest scientific breakthroughs, techniques and theories, as well as hiring and directing scientists and lab workers at the laboratory and scrounging up new business deals. She often traveled to speak with clients or to agronomic research conferences.

As Larissa's company grew, so did her waistline and jowls, but just as no amount of expensive clothing could hide her expanding girth, nothing in the world could stop Larissa's obnoxious behavior. Larissa got used to being the boss at her company, and she wanted her family to treat her the same way. She belittled her husband in front of guests, made fun of his impotency problems, bragged about an affair she had, and often boasted she made more money than him. It is not as if Tim worked at a gas station—he earned almost eighty thousand dollars a year at the hospital, which is a lot of money to be had in Fresno, where 26 percent of the population lives below the national poverty rate.

The relationship between Larissa and her daughter got problematic as Kristin entered her teenage years, and the two had frequent yelling matches at their Clovis home. Instead of coming to an understanding or seeing a guidance counselor, Larissa sent Kristin to live with her parents in the hinterlands of Clarence, Missouri. By 2002, it became obvious to all of their friends and acquaintances that the Schusters' marriage was on the rocks.

The couple filed for divorce, but still lived together in their sprawling home, albeit in separate sections of the house. Larissa acted as if she were the sole owner of the home and harped on Tim relentlessly. While Larissa visited her family in Missouri over the 2002 Fourth of July holiday, Tim moved out of the house and into a condo.

Larissa blew her top when she got home and discovered Tim had moved out. She became even angrier that Tim took some household objects with him, as if he had no ownership of anything collected during their twenty-one years together. Tim also held firm in the divorce proceedings over the distribution of their joint property, which drove Larissa crazy.

Larissa got custody over Tyler, with Tim having custody every other weekend. They arranged their meet-up place where Larissa got her nails done. Inevitably Larissa would start yelling obscenities at Tim until he drove off. Larissa would let loose a tirade of insults concerning her ex-husband, especially his virility. Once, after a particularly bad exchange, Larissa told her longtime manicurist, Terri Lopez, that she wanted Tim dead and that she could do it and get away with it. Not long afterward, Larissa had an employee, chemist Leslie Fichera, rent out a nearby storage place in Fichera's name. She gave the keys and entry code to Larissa who told Fichera she wanted to use the storage space to hide property she did not want Tim to have.

Sometime before August 10, 2002, Larissa, along with another employee, twenty-one-year-old James Fagone, broke into Tim's condo while he was on a short vacation. She removed items she felt belonged to her and ransacked the rest of the place. After discovering the break-in, Tim knew Larissa committed the crime, but decided not to get the police involved. Instead, he moved to a home in Clovis and had it rigged with security lights, motion sensors, and cameras. He also bought a gun and secured a conceal weapon permit.

Larissa Schuster had a big mouth that would eventually get the best of her. She thought nothing of leaving long, obscenity-laden messages and threats on Tim's telephone message machine. She started asking her employees and acquaintances if they would beat up or kill Tim. For some reason, Larissa told her long-suffering manicurist that she prayed every night Tim would die.

On April 30, 2003, a fifty-five-gallon blue plastic barrel was delivered to Central California Research Labs. It was not a barrel that the lab would usually order for their business. Larissa told her warehouse staff she planned to use it as a compost bin at her home, but then asked them if they thought a body would fit into the barrel. The employees laughed it off, but Larissa was not joking.

The lab had on hand various types of acids—acetic, hydrochloric, and sulfuric—but they were never bought in volume as the lab did not have a need for them. Eyebrows were raised in the shipping and receiving department of Central California Research Labs when between June 13 and July 2, three cases of hydrochloric and one case of sulfuric acid was delivered to C.C.R.L. The shipping and receiving clerks were confounded by the order as the lab used only a couple of liters of the acids a year, but the chemicals had been personally ordered by Larissa, so they signed and stored them as procedure called for. Not long afterward, Larissa's neighbors noticed a large blue barrel was delivered to her home.

In the early morning hours of July 10, 2003, Larissa called Tim at his home and told him she was injured and outside his home. When Tim stepped outside Fagone overpowered him and incapacitated him using a stun gun. Fagone dragged Tim back into the house and rendered him unconscious with chloroform. They tied Tim up, tossed him into the back of his pickup truck, and drove to Larissa's home.

In her garage, Larissa Schuster and Fagone dumped Tim headfirst into the barrel and poured eleven gallons of hydrochloric and three gallons of sulfuric acid into the barrel and over her unconscious ex-husband, the father of her children. It did not bother Larissa Schuster that Tim was still alive as they poured the caustic solutions over his body and sealed the barrel.

Schuster, being the belligerent, self-centered person she was, never thought her ex-husband would be missed. She was so self-absorbed in her having complete ownership of C.C.R.L., she did not know that Tim had been laid off from his job at the hospital during the week. His friend and coworker, Mary Solis had been laid off too, and they arranged to have breakfast together that morning to discuss their shared experience. Tim never missed an appointment. After Tim did not answer his phone, Solis called a mutual friend, Victor Uribe. Victor drove to Tim's home and discovered the door unlocked. Inside, he found Tim's cell phone, wallet, and watch. He knew Tim would never leave his home without those three things.

To keep up appearances, Larissa took her son Tyler to the usual meeting spot at her nail salon so he could spend the weekend with his father. Larissa was upbeat and chatty with manicurist Terri Lopez, telling her, "I have a feeling the divorce is going to go my way." Meanwhile, Tyler stood outside the salon in the unbearably hot Fresno summer heat waiting for his father, whom he would never see again.

Mary Solis, still concerned about the whereabouts of Tim, called the nail salon to ask Lopez if he had been there to pick up Tyler. When Lopez resumed working on Schuster's nails, she found that Larissa's hands were so sweaty that the glue used to attach her acrylic fingernails would not dry properly.

The next day, Bob and Mary Solis called the Clovis police to report Tim's disappearance. Because of Tim's recent divorce and unemployment, the police did not think much of the case. He could have gone to Yosemite, Sequoia or Kings Canyon National Parks, which are east of Fresno, or he could have gone to Las Vegas to blow off steam. Checking out the report, Detectives Vince Weibert and Larry Kirkhart arrived at the scene and when they checked the messages on Tim's phone answering machine, they were stunned by the vile voice messages Larissa had left. Tim had saved all of his voice messages from Larissa to help his case when the couple split up their communal property. The detectives noted all the phone calls to Tim's cell phone from Larissa. One call from Larissa in the early morning hours of July 10, really piqued their interest. They called Larissa and asked her to come to the police department to talk to them about her missing ex-husband.

When Larissa came in for the interview that evening, she denied having called Tim. She told detectives she must have accidently hit the speed dial and called him without knowing it. She admitted that they were in the middle of a heated divorce, but so were a lot of other couples.

The detectives asked Schuster if she had her telephone with her, and she declared she had not brought it with her. Detectives Weibert and Kirkhart told Schuster she could leave, and they walked her to her car. Spotting Schuster's phone inside her car, they took a look at it to see if she had Tim on speed dial. If he was on her speed dial, then she could have accidently called him. If not, her story would not hold up. Tim was not on her speed dial. They looked closely at her call log and noticed the name James Fagone. They also noticed abrasions on Larissa's legs. With nothing else to go on, they let her go on her way.

Schuster called Fagone when she left the police station and told him to meet her at her home. They loaded the barrel onto the bed of a rented truck and drove to the storage unit. Popping open the lid, they were hit by the repulsive stench of hydrochloric acid and dissolved human flesh. To make more room in the barrel, Schuster cut off Tim Schuster's feet and then poured in three more bottles of acid, before they resealed the barrel.

Larissa had planned a vacation with Tyler to start the next day. They were first going to go to Disney World in Orlando, then to Missouri to visit her family. While she was out of town, Detectives Weibert and Kirkhart looked up Fagone to ask him questions about his relationship with Schuster, and if he knew where Tim had gone. The two streetwise detectives knew they could sweat the truth out of the twenty-one-year-old. Each time the detectives interviewed Fagone, he told more than he should have until, during the third interview, he admitted to being paid two thousand dollars by Larissa for helping with the murder. He told police he had ditched the stun gun in a portable toilet at a construction site. Once the stun gun was recovered, they knew Fagone told the truth. The detectives secured search warrants for all of Larissa Schuster's property, including her business and the storage locker that had been leased in her employees' name.

The police recoiled at the rank odor emitting from the storage unit. After moving boxes around, they discovered the blue, fifty-five-gallon sealed barrel, which upon opening released a stomach-emptying stench that spread throughout the complex. Even more sickening were the remains of Timothy Schuster, forty-five-year-old father of two, Mason, nurse, and all-around nice guy. His legs and hips were the only parts of his body not dissolved by the acid.

Police put out arrest warrants for Fagone and Schuster. Fagone was arrested at his parents' home, and after some quick investigating, detectives learned Schuster planned to fly into St. Louis that day. Local police arrested Schuster when she departed the airplane in St. Louis. She, like Fagone, was charged with first degree murder.

On November 27, 2006, James Fagone went on trial, and he blamed everything on Schuster. He claimed he did not know Tim would be murdered, and only did what Schuster told him to do. He tried to recant his confession after the prosecution showed the jury his videotaped confession. On December 12, 2006, Fagone was found guilty of first degree murder and given life without parole.

Schuster and her attorney, Roger Nuttall used every trick in the book to delay and derail her trial before it finally took place on October 22, 2007, in Los Angeles County Superior Court in Van Nuys. James Fagone appealed his conviction and refused to participate in Schuster's trial. The prosecution could not use Fagone's taped confession because her attorney could not cross-examine him, but the prosecution had motive and plenty of circumstantial evidence to go through with the trial. It also helped that Schuster had so openly spoken of her hatred for her ex-husband and there was no shortage of witnesses willing to testify to that.

The prosecution brought out employees of Central California Research Labs who testified to the massive order of hydrochloric and sulfuric acid ordered by Schuster. They also swore to the fifty-five-gallon blue plastic barrel the lab had never ordered before, and how she asked one witness if he thought that a body would fit into it. Leslie Fichera told the court about Larissa having her rent the storage unit in her name, and giving her the keys and the security code. Another employee testified to renting a truck in his name for Larissa the day the barrel was moved to the storage unit.

Police detectives told the court about the two dozen vile and threatening phone messages they discovered on Timothy's answering machine, the phone records to Timothy, and how they found the dust outline of the barrel in her garage. They told of finding the barrel in the storage unit, and the sequence of uncovering the partially dissolved body of Timothy Schuster. The prosecution played the two -hour interview Schuster had with Clovis police.

The prosecution brought up the messy divorce and Larissa's refusal to split up the community property, including Central California Research Labs, which was worth several million dollars. By California law, married couples split fifty-fifty any income or property earned or acquired during their marriage.

Family friend Bob Solis gave his account of Larissa's derogatory tirades against her husband. Larissa's hair stylist, Becky Holland, told the court about her client raving about getting even with her husband. Despite the reality that listening to her various clients complain about their divorces was an inevitable part of her job, Larissa's dark rants made Holland uncomfortable. Terri Lopez took the stand and backed up Holland's testimony and told how upbeat, but sweaty, Larissa was on July 10.

The defense made a show of the case, claiming James Fagone had murdered Tim and that the two thousand dollars she had paid him was for when Fagone had babysat her son Tyler. The defense brought up some character witnesses who made the murderer sound like the nicest person from Clovis since actor Ken Curtis, who played Festus on the long-running television program *Gunsmoke* and who moved to Clovis after the show was cancelled.

Then Larissa Schuster regally took the stand to provide her Academy Award–worthy testimony. Charming and articulate, Schuster kept her wits and her temper at bay as she went through two days of cross-examination. She had an excuse for everything, from the unusual purchases at the lab, to her foul-mouth messages left on Tim's answering machine. The only thing she admitted was helping Fagone move the barrel to the storage unit.

On December 12, 2007, exactly one year to the day of James Fagone's conviction, the jury convicted Larissa Schuster of first degree murder. Schuster sat impassive while Timothy's friends and family raucously celebrated in the courtroom.

On May 16, 2008, Larissa Schuster was sentenced to life without parole. Seven people, including daughter Kristin and Tim's mother, Shirley, gave a victim-impact statement at the sentencing. Throughout the tearful statements, Larissa remained stone-faced.

Oh My Mama

September 15, 1944—Diamond Springs
Murderer: Winifred Cox
Victim: Mary Cox

World War II had everyone on edge. Even in the pastoral foothills of the Sierra Nevada mountains, uneasiness hung in the air. Virtually every family felt the effects of the war, as fathers, sons, and brothers were either in uniform or working for the war effort in the shipyards, factories, and fields. Many families were split up, and to some it proved too much to handle.

Fifty-four-year-old Mary Cox was troubled. The Diamond Springs mother had been institutionalized for three weeks during the summer, and was a mental wreck.

On September 15, 1944, while her husband Charles worked at the nearby California Door Company, Mary barged into the bathroom of her home and attacked her bathing daughter, Winifred, with a baseball bat. Winnie managed to wrestle the bat away from her mother, but not before being hit in the head several times. Dazed and naked in the tub, Winnie was trying to get her wits about her when Mary barged into the bathroom again, this time with a small camping axe. She hit Winnie over the head with the axe while yelling, "Why won't you die?" Winnie feigned death to make her mother stop. She had read that Marines were told to do that if they were overrun by the enemy. When that did not work, Winnie told her mother that using a gun would be easier. Mary agreed and helped the fourteen-year-old honor student out of the tub. Mary brought Winnie's clothes and dressed her daughter's wounds. The pair retrieved her father's powerful 30-30 rifle, but could not load it. Taking a .20 gauge shotgun instead, they went into the bathroom. Standing against the wall in the small room, Mary took the barrel of the shotgun, put the end of the barrel to her face, and asked the dazed and bleeding Winnie to shoot her. She did. Weak from the beating and loss of blood, Winnie collapsed on the living room sofa, and was found by her father when he came home for lunch.

Winnie was cleared of all charges.

Going Postal

January 30, 2006—5200 Overpass Road, Santa Barbara, and
400 Storke Road, Goleta
Murderer: Jennifer San Marco
Victims: Beverly Graham, Ze Fairchild, Maleka Higgins, Nicola Grant,
Guadalupe Swartz, Dexter Shannon, and Charlotte Colton

It has always been shameful the way humans treat the mentally ill. Up until the reign of President Reagan, the federal government funded mental health programs throughout the United States. In 1980, newly elected Reagan and his conservative Republicans discarded the Mental Health Systems Act that President Jimmy Carter had signed, essentially defunding mental health institutions all over America. Those with mental illnesses suddenly found themselves on their own as asylums, sanitariums and institutions shut their doors. The neediest of these people ended up on the streets, homeless and insane. But not all of the mentally ill are homeless, unemployable maniacs in dirty clothes pushing a shopping cart full of found objects. Many of them started out like anyone else, before mental illness took over their lives.

There had to be a time in Jennifer San Marco's life where she had a grip on reality. Jennifer was born in New York City on December 6, 1961, and attended Brooklyn's Edward R. Murrow High School, whose former students includes the late artist Jean-Michel Basquiat, the late rap musician Adam Yauch of the Beastie Boys, and Academy Award–winning actress Marisa Tomei. She later attended Brooklyn College and Rutgers University before she dropped out and moved to California in 1989 with her husband.

San Marco found work right away as a prison guard at a medium-security prison, but quit without giving notice just two days before her employment probation period ended. She went on to a job as a police dispatcher for the Santa Barbara Police Department. She passed all the psychological exams and an extensive background check for the position, but she quit after a few months, lasting about as long as most people who do that stressful job.

By 1997, a divorced San Marco worked the graveyard shift at the massive United States Postal Service sorting plant in Goleta, outside of Santa Barbara. It has been widely documented how stressful working at these large sorting facilities are for some people. The term "Going Postal" is a direct result of the rash of workplace massacres that occurred at letter sorting plants and post office buildings starting in 1983.

By 2003, San Marco showed signs of becoming unbalanced. She started talking to herself, which is not unusual in a large, machine-filled building. The loneliness of operating a massive mail-sorting machine is indescribable. The rattling noise of the sorting machines, which route mail along and are basically a small model rail train set, is unrelenting and it rarely ever stops. The job itself is monotonous, watching for jams on a sixty foot

clanking moving track of envelopes. The only way you can communicate with a fellow worker is visually. Some operators recite lines from films, rehearse what they want to tell someone, or sing. Combine the noise, monotony, and loneliness with a person in a fragile psychological state, and you have a recipe for a mental illness disaster.

In early 2001, San Marco's fellow postal workers started to complain to their supervisors and union steward about San Marco muttering racial slurs. Much like someone with Tourette's Syndrome, she was talking to herself, not her coworkers. Her fellow postal employees could see her at her station carrying on an argument with herself, and they began to fear her erratic behavior. Removed from the shop floor, San Marco received some time off. She sought out a mental health specialist.

During this time Jennifer started to annoy her neighbors in her condominium complex at 5200 Overpass Road in Santa Barbara. She liked to walk into the common area and sing at the top of her lungs at random times during the day and night. San Marco would get into loud arguments with herself on her front step and then greet a neighbor as if she had not been screaming seconds before. Neighbor Beverly Graham did not put up with such behavior and would regularly confront San Marco about her disruptive conduct, yelling to her out of a window to "shut up."

Things came to a head in February 2003 when her behavior had disturbed her coworkers to the point that they were all terrified of her. The police arrived and removed San Marco from the Goleta annex. She was handcuffed and hogtied on a wheeled cart used to move bags of mail. They brought San Marco to a hospital for a mental health observation and evaluation. The USPO gave her indefinite medical disability leave.

San Marco sold her Santa Barbara condo, and told neighbors she was going back east to visit her family. She made it as far as Grants, New Mexico, when her car broke down, and she decided Grants was as good of a place as any to live.

Grants is about eighty miles west of Albuquerque, and is the county seat of Cibola County. Interstate 40 and the famous Route 66 go right through Grants. Uranium mining used to be the basis of the area's economy, but that ended in the 1980s. With a population of less than ten thousand mostly Hispanic residents, San Marco stood out like a boat in the desert. She wasted little time in becoming Grants' resident crazy lady.

San Marco got a place to live and raised eyebrows at city hall when she applied for a business license for a newsletter she wanted to publish called "The Racists Press." San Marco was fond of kneeling in prayer alongside streets or in parking lots. Sometimes she would get other people to join her. One incident involved San Marco showing up at a gas station naked, but by the time police came she was clothed.

San Marco, her appearance becoming more and more unkempt, became a fixture at city hall after officials rejected her license to start a cat food company because she lived outside the city limits. She would stare at one employee in particular. It disturbed the employee enough that coworkers warned her when San Marco entered the building.

On January 30, 2006, San Marco showed up in Santa Barbara and paid her old next door neighbor Beverly Graham a visit with a 9 mm Smith & Wesson model 915. Leaving Graham's body on the floor of her home, San Marco drove to her former place of employment, the United States Postal Service sorting plant in nearby Goleta.

Forty-four-year-old San Marco drove through the gate of the compound by closely following the vehicle in front of her. She shot and killed two people in the parking lot and took an employee's identification badge at gunpoint to gain entry to the annex. The shooting started immediately and dozens of postal employees ran out of the building.

When it was over, Jennifer San Marco had shot and killed Dexter Shannon, Maleka Higgins, Guadalupe Swartz, Nicola Grant, Charlotte Colton, and Ze Fairchild before putting the gun to her own head and pulling the trigger. None of the victims had a clue they were going to be shot in the head by a person they most likely had almost forgotten about. Out of the six postal workers murdered that day by Jennifer San Marco, three were African-American, one was Chinese-American, one was Mexican-American and another was Filipino-American. They were between twenty-eight and fifty-seven-years-old. The body of Beverly Graham was found the next day.

Police traced the gun that San Marco used to a New Mexico pawn shop. San Marco passed the background check and was able to pick up her pistol after a two-day waiting period. When police searched San Marco's home in Grants, New Mexico, they found notebooks full of the ramblings of an insane person and not much else.

Really Bad Mom

August 7, 2007—Camino Bello, Rowland Heights
Murderer: Man-Ling Williams
Victim: Devon, Ian, and Neal Williams

Some people are not cut out for the restrictions and rigors of parenthood. Most of the time it is the male who ditches his family for lack of interest or heart, and in most societies that is acceptable. Males are expendable, like bucks in the forest or soldiers in a battlefield. It is rare that the female leaves her home and family, and it is even rarer when a mother kills her children in order to be single again.

Man-Ling Tsang grew up in the Los Angeles bedroom community of Hacienda Heights and graduated from Los Altos High School in 1998. The community of fifty-four thousand is home to mostly middle class Caucasians, Asians, and Hispanics, as well as to the Hsi Lai Temple, the largest Buddhist Temple in North America. With the exception of a handful of athletes, musicians, and a porn actor or two, no one of any renown hails from Hacienda Heights. It is just another eastern San Gabriel Valley suburb that seamlessly blends into the next suburb.

Tsang met Neal Williams when they were teenagers. After high school, they started dating and Tsang became pregnant. The couple married, had their son Devon, and four years later had another boy, Ian. They lived in a condo on Camino Bello, a block-long street of identical shoddy dwellings built in the early 1980s as apartments in Rowland Heights. Ironically, Camino Bello is Spanish for Beautiful Road. The couple lived a somewhat normal life, as least as far as Neal and the boys were concerned, but Man-Ling felt different. She seldom garnered satisfaction being a mother and wife.

While Neal and the children were friendly and well-liked on their street, others considered Man-Ling a foul-mouthed, ornery slob. She rarely spoke to neighbors, and when she did it was in Mandarin to Chinese-Americans, and only a simple greeting. She often chain-smoked on their front step and neighbors reported hearing the couple argue and slam doors.

To help make ends meet and to get out of the house, Man-Ling waitressed at a Marie Callender's Restaurant in nearby La Puente. Man-Ling

never shied away from telling her coworkers how miserable her life felt. She lamented she wasted her youth, and thought she deserved a better life than she had. She had never lived any farther than a few miles from Hacienda Heights.

In June 2007, Man-Ling met up with some old high school friends for dinner. One of the alumni was John Gregory, who Man-Ling stayed in contact with through the Internet afterwards. In July, Man-Ling contacted Gregory, who lived in Santa Barbara, to inform him she planned to be in Santa Barbara that month and would like to see him. Man-Ling told Neal that she was going to a Marie Callender's training seminar in Santa Barbara for the weekend. There was no seminar, and Gregory and Man-Ling had sex over the weekend, but like everything in Man-Ling's life, there were no sparks. Man-Ling and Gregory maturely agreed to be friends and leave it as that.

August 7, 2007, was a hot Tuesday night in the San Gabriel Valley. The air hung stagnated with carbons emitted from internal combustion engines. Man-Ling was home alone with three-year-old Ian and seven-year-old Devon. She ordered a pizza for dinner and then put them to bed. After waiting for them to fall asleep, she smothered the brothers in their bunk beds with a pillow. It takes between five to ten minutes to suffocate someone. Man-Ling had that much time to think about what she was doing while murdering her own children.

When Neal came home an hour later, Man-Ling attacked him with a twenty-inch katana sword. As a hobby, Neal collected swords and he took good care of them, keeping them honed enough to cut paper. Man-Ling, wearing latex gloves, went to work on her husband by slashing and stabbing him over ninety-seven times. He put up as much of a fight as a defenseless man could when faced with a samurai-type sword. He had twenty-two defensive wounds on his hands. Two of his fingers were sliced off. One wound went through from his neck and out to his back. Getting speared in the heart sealed his ticket to death. To make sure Neal was dead, Man-Ling chopped at the back of Neal's neck, severing the spinal cord and fracturing the base of his skull. Man-Ling was not done with her husband and the father of her now dead children. She continued to stab, chop and slice Neal's torso. The medical examiner later testified that it took approximately ten minutes for Neal Williams to bleed out and die.

Man-Ling removed her blood-soaked clothes and took a shower. Tip-toeing to avoid getting her husband's blood on her shoes, Man-Ling left the house and went to a TGI Fridays Restaurant for drinks with her coworkers from Marie Callender's.

Coming home in the early morning hours, Man-Ling pretended to discover her butchered husband's body. Running and screaming around her yard, she woke up everyone on Camino Bello. The police were called and pajama-clad neighbors stepped outside of their homes in the still, hot night, shocked that a murder could happen on their little street.

The police noticed that Man-Ling was crying, but there were no tears. When she retrieved her cigarettes from her car, detectives noticed blood on the cellophane wrapper covering the pack of Camels. Man-Ling cracked like an egg when detectives asked about the bloody cigarette pack and admitted to the murders. At the jail, the police discovered specks of Neal's blood on her shoes and brassiere.

Police charged Man-Ling Williams with three counts of first degree murder. The case was prosecuted by Los Angeles County Deputy District Attorneys Stacy Okun-Wiese and Pak Kouch, and presided over by Pomona Superior Court Judge Robert Martinez. Man-Lin's flimsy defense that she felt trapped in a lifestyle that did not interest her did not hold up in court.

On January 18, 2012, almost four years after the murders of Neal, Ian, and Devon Williams, Judge Martinez sentenced Man-Ling Williams to death.

Lost Little Girl

July 21, 1947—1310 Bruceville Road, Elk Grove
Murderer: Louise Gomes
Victim: Mary Lou Roman

Before 1980, the Sacramento suburb of Elk Grove was just a crossroad with a store, a grain elevator, and a railroad depot, a far cry from the cookie-cutter burb of 160,000 people it had become by 2010. Before the arrival of the Europeans in 1808, the rich loam near the once constantly shifting confluence of the Consumnes and Sacramento rivers made the area a virtual Garden of Eden. Cottonwood and live oak trees covered the area like beach umbrellas. The water was abundant with fish, and the woods were filled with the singing of birds. Of course, there were plenty of elk around, too. In 1776, Native Americans ambushed a squad of conquistadors and murdered them at the confluence of the Consumnes and Sacramento rivers.

In 1947, Elk Grove could have been one hundred miles away from Sacramento. On July 21, not far from Elk Grove Corner, fourteen-year-old Louise Gomes finished washing the lunchtime dishes with ten-year-old Mary Lou Roman, who boarded at Gomes's house. Gomes's parents, Charles and his wife, went shopping and left the studious bookworm Louise to keep an eye on her two-year-old brother Jerry, nine-year-old sister Barbara Jean, Mary Lou, and their invalid grandfather Charles Senior. After finishing their chores, Mary Lou and Louise sat outside on the back doorstep. The two started arguing and in a fit of anger Louise started choking Mary Lou. Fighting for her life, Mary Lou fell to the ground. Louise picked up a lead jack handle and beat the ten-year-old over the head. Seeing Mary Lou still breathing, Louise walked to the front of the house, past her invalid grandfather who sat on the front porch, picked up a three-pound sledgehammer, and carried it to the backyard. She finished off Mary Lou with the stone sledge. Louise changed out of her blood-splattered clothes and cleaned up. Then she waited for the fireworks to begin.

Mary Lou's body was found by Wilda Eagan, who had stopped by the Gomes's farm with oranges to sell. Without saying anything, she quietly left the farm and hurried to the nearest neighbor and told him what she saw.

The police were called, and Louise immediately admitted she murdered Mary Lou Roman. When Grandpa Gomes heard about the murder, he suffered a stroke.

Louise Gomes was unapologetic about murdering her foster sister. She told Sacramento County Sheriff Don Cox she had wanted to kill someone for a year, and had previously killed rabbits and cats for pleasure. At first she wanted to kill her mother, then little Jerry, and even Barbara Jean, until she settled on the lodger Mary Lou.

Dry-eyed and calm, she told the stunned lawman, "Yes I did it, but I don't know why."

Louise was born March 9, 1933, in San Francisco and was given up for adoption on August 26 of that year. Charles and his wife ran a certified foster home at their desolate farm not far from Elk Grove Corner, and subsidized their income by boarding or taking in foster children. Mary Lou boarded at the Gomes' while her father worked at a Stockton sanitarium. To give you an idea of what kind of parents the Gomes were, when asked by a reporter from the *Sacramento Bee* about how could an honor student like Louise commit such a crime, the couple replied, "Louise must be a mental case."

Louise was candid with Sheriff Cox, and she had not an ounce of remorse about her crime. "Now I feel relieved all over. I have accomplished my desire." When asked if she felt bad about killing the little girl, Louise replied, "I'm not sorry when anyone dies. I only cry when I get a whipping."

Louise Gomes was sentenced on October 14, 1947, to the state mental hospital at Pacific Colony until a time when officials deemed she no longer posed a danger to anyone. On June 21, 1955, at the age of twenty-one, Louise was removed from a foster home in Nevada City and sent to the Women's State Prison at Corona. The authorities said it was to prevent another murder by the young woman.

The Doctor's Wife, Part IV

December 4, 2010—3750 Grim Avenue, Apt. 2, North Park, San Diego
Murderer: Jennifer Trayers
Victim: Lt. Cmdr. Frederick Trayers

Love is an odd thing. It is impossible to describe without falling into cliché metaphors, but love is more than an emotion, and it is what drives most of us through our day. When everything in life is stripped down to nuts and bolts, love is all that matters.

Jennifer Smith met the athletic Frederick Trayers while they were students at the University of Notre Dame in South Bend, Indiana. Trayers liked to chat with Jennifer while she was at her job as a travel agent. They quickly fell in love. Trayers, who had enlisted in the Navy, went off to flight school in Pensacola, Florida, after graduation. The couple had a long distance relationship, and when Trayers found out he was to be stationed in San Diego, the two eloped in December 1992. They renewed their vows and had a proper wedding reception in November 1993 in front of friends and family back in Indiana. Jennifer was happy to be a military wife.

In 2002, the couple moved to Fort Lauderdale, Florida, so Fred could attend medical school at Nova Southeastern University. Jennifer got a job at a timeshare company. During this time, both of them had extramarital affairs, and like many couples, they were able to put their marriage back together.

By the time Fred graduated from medical school in 2005 he had achieved the rank of Lieutenant Commander, and his first assignment as a military doctor was at Camp Pendleton in Oceanside, California. The couple bought a home and by all accounts lived a tranquil, normal life. Doc Trayers earned the respect of his colleagues by not only his skills as a doctor, but also for his calm and professional manner. Jennifer worked at a bank. In 2007 the couple hosted a party celebrating their fifteenth wedding anniversary. In 2010, Fred received orders to report to Balboa Naval Hospital in San Diego, thirty-eight miles south of Oceanside. The couple rented out their home and moved to an apartment at 3750 Grim Avenue in the North Park section of San Diego. Jennifer transferred to a nearby branch of her bank and everyone seemed happy.

Not long after the transfer, Lt. Cmdr. Trayers was called to sea. He arrived in Australia to report to the USNS *Mercy*, a hospital ship on a humanitarian mission called "Pacific Partnership 2012." The *Mercy* traveled the South Pacific, tending to the medical needs of people in Vietnam, Cambodia, Indonesia, Guam, and Timor.

While the USNS *Mercy* sailed the South Pacific and anchored at exotic ports of call, Doc Trayers and Ensign Danielle Robins, a beautiful navy physician ten years younger than him, became attached to one another. Not only was Lt. Cmdr. Trayers her superior officer, but the United State Navy has a rule about officers committing adultery, especially with lower ranking officers. If caught, the offenders can be demoted or even discharged from the Navy. Their careers ruined, their pensions gone. They would be lucky to write prescriptions for medical marijuana or work at a clinic treating sexually transmitted diseases.

After the mission, the Navy transferred Ensign Robins to Balboa Naval Hospital in San Diego, where she and Doc Trayers resumed their sexual, tension-filled relationship. This did not go unnoticed by Jennifer. She saw little things that tipped her off, such as lots of text messaging and emailing, and how Fred went directly to the shower when he came home in the morning from working the night shift. They started to see a marriage counselor but it did little good. Upset, Jennifer started to lose weight and slept little. As a fraud investigator for a major Southern California bank, it wasn't Jennifer's job to dole out cash and take deposits. She was up to date on the latest spyware and other crafty ways to look up people's records and emails without the user knowing. Jennifer downloaded a spyware tracking program onto her husband's laptop computer and started to monitor his online activity.

On the morning of December 4, 2010, Jennifer, using her husband's email account, contacted Ensign Robins and sent her an epic eight-page message with the title "Mr. Wonderful." Jennifer raved about her eighteen years of marriage, and listed the doctor's good and bad traits. She taunted Ensign Robins, informing her of the married couple's recent sex life. She ended the tirade with this ominous line: "You should feel guilty now! You just ruined the marriage of a wonderful man! The career of a wonderful man! The future of a wonderful man! Sincerely, Mrs. Wonderful."

When the doctor came home that morning from his graveyard shift at the hospital, he took some cold medicine and went to bed. Jennifer had not been sleeping for days, and wanted to have a serious talk about their marriage. Fred just wanted to sleep. Jennifer climbed into bed with her husband, took out a butcher knife and superficially cut her wrist. When she poked herself in the stomach, Fred reached over to the nightstand, opened a drawer and produced a large military knife called a Ka-Bar. "Here," he told Jennifer, "use this."

Jennifer took the Ka-Bar and stabbed herself in the chest several times, Fred grabbed the knife and the two wrestled for control. When the doctor reached over toward the nightstand, Jennifer thought that he was grabbing the butcher knife, so she stabbed him in the back of his neck. With every stab, Jennifer released the anger and frustration that had built up in her marriage over their nearly twenty years together. The sacrifices she made being a military wife with the cross-country transfers, assignments that took him away from home for months at a time, and the nightshifts and weekends he usually worked. Add the affairs, the lies, and their decision to put off having a family until a time that never came and before she knew it, Jennifer had stabbed her husband eleven times.

She had inflicted fatal wounds to his heart, kidneys and lungs. The doctor lay sprawled on the floor next to the blood-soaked bed, dead.

For the next two days, Jennifer stayed in the bloody bedroom with her lifeless husband, poking at herself with the Ka-Bar, trying to die from a thousand cuts—and she almost succeeded had it not been for the Navy being concerned that an officer had not reported for duty for two days. Jennifer was found close to death and taken to the hospital. Lieutenant Commander Frederick Trayers, M.D., was taken to the morgue. While in her hospital room, recovering from over two dozen superficial cuts and loss of blood, police charged Jennifer with first degree murder.

Jennifer Trayers's two-week-long trial started on January 23, 2012. She claimed to be emotionally distraught over the affair her husband carried on with Ensign Robins and did not know what she was doing. Ensign Robins took the witness stand and told the jury she was emotionally attached to Fred, but they did not have a sexual relationship.

The jury deliberated for three days and on February 8, 2012, found Jennifer Trayers guilty of second-degree murder. A judge sentenced her to 16 years to life in prison.

An Arm and a Leg

April 20, 2011—23711 Meadow Falls Drive, Diamond Bar
Murderer: Carmen Montelongo, aka Carmen Montenegro
Victim: Samuel Wiggins

For many, Diamond Bar, Riverside, Bell Gardens, Ontario, Rancho, Cucamonga, Chino, or Fontana are merely names on freeway signs in East Los Angeles and Riverside County. This middle class slice of Los Angeles is where everyday people live everyday lives. They go to work, do some barbecuing, and work on their home improvement projects, but some crave to have more. One of the most realistic opportunities for a person of modest means to earn more money is to buy real estate. A couple of rental properties can be a good investment, but it won't make you rich, and neither will killing your boyfriend.

Riverside resident Carmen Montelongo, who also went by Carmen Montenegro, and listed her age as both forty-five and fifty-one years old, dated retired Boeing employee Samuel Wiggins for a couple of years. Wiggins, a sixty-two-year-old lifelong bachelor saw something in Montelongo that Wiggins's family could not see. They thought she took advantage of Wiggins, and she did, but with Wiggins's approval. He let Montelongo and her daughter, Chanel Alicia Ortiz, live with him for a time at his modest Diamond Bar home. Wiggins, a Vietnam War veteran who grew up in Compton, also helped Ortiz pay her college tuition. He knew Montelongo stole small things like compact discs, but he did not care. In fact, he told his nephew that he planned on marrying Montelongo.

No one saw Samuel Wiggins during the last part of April 2011, and when his family telephoned the house at 23711 Meadow Falls Drive, Montelongo answered and made up an excuse that Sam was out of town for a few days. They did not believe her and rightfully so, because on April 20, Carmen stabbed Wiggins twice in the chest and twenty-two times in the back. She hacked up his body and buried it in her grandmother's backyard twenty miles east of Diamond Bar in the city of Ontario. During the last weeks of April and most of May, Montelongo raided Wiggins's checking, savings, and money-market bank accounts. She drove around East Los Angeles County in Wiggins's 2009 Honda Accord, using his credit cards on a spending

spree that lasted until she reached his credit limit. Wiggins's family kept the police updated on Montelongo's activity.

By May, the police started nosing around asking questions, Montelongo felt the heat. She drove to her grandmother's home at 735 North Holmes Avenue in Ontario, dug up Wiggins's head and arms, put them into two large flower pots, covered them with dirt and planted an ornamental patio plant on top. She enlisted her son, twenty-five-year-old Daniel Ortiz, to unwittingly help her, sending him to a relative's home at 6726 Foster Bridge Road in Bell Gardens, with the large potted plants as a late Mother's Day gift.

It all came to a screeching halt for Montelongo on May 29, after Carmen's cousin discovered her and two day-laborers digging up the reeking torso of Samuel Wiggins at their grandmother's home. Panicked, the day-laborers ran to their pickup truck, sped off, and were never seen or heard from again. Montelongo offered her cousin five thousand dollars to help her get rid of Wiggins. He violently vomited, and then called the police, as did several neighbors who either witnessed the incident or were sickened by the putrid fumes that hung over the neighborhood like a wet dog blanket.

Riverside County sheriff's deputies found Carmen Montelongo a few doors down from her grandmother's home at the corner of H Street and Holmes Avenue pushing a thirty-gallon plastic garbage container. Samuel Wiggins' rotted rib cage and sawed-off legs were inside the trash can. He was identified through fingerprints, dentures, and his distinctive surgical scars.

A jury found Carmen Montelongo guilty of first degree murder. She is now serving twenty-six years to life in prison.

Not So Happy Campers

February–April 1948—Sonora
Murderer: Ada Peters Hansen
Victim: Otto Hansen

Forty-one-year-old, twice-widowed Ada Peters Hansen and her common-law husband, forty-five-year old Otto Hansen, were down on their luck. The couple bided their time, spending the winter living in a resort cabin at a campground outside of Sonora. Their four-thousand-dollar nest egg was gone. They had planned on using the money to open a bar in Alaska, but Otto gradually lost the cash playing cards at the campground store.

In early March 1948, Ada told the manager of the auto park that Otto went to Idaho to look for work. Ada stayed at the cabin, picking up odd jobs here and there. She arose some suspicion on April 26 when she applied for the authority to cash Otto's unemployment checks. On July 15, Ada moved out of the campground, telling the manager she got a job for the summer at the Cliff House near Groveland.

Summer came, and so did the tourists. On August 16, 1948, while enjoying their stay at the cabin that Ada and Otto had lived in, the family who leased the cabin noticed a putrid odor coming out of the dirt on the side of the building, and after poking around they discovered two shallow graves. One grave contained Otto's head, legs and arms. Six feet away was Otto's torso.

Police captured Ada on August 18 at a beauty parlor in Modesto. She first told the officers that Otto was in Alaska, and then she said his body was dumped at the door of their cabin, and finally she claimed that Otto was ill and begged her to give him poison to end his misery. She fed him the poison and left his body in the cabin for two days while she went about her life. She finally took a boning knife and a hatchet to cut Otto's body up. She buried the torso under a foot of dirt. The rest of him she buried only six to eight inches deep. She mopped up the bloody floor and then threw away the mop. A couple of days later she ordered three sacks of top soil and some lime. She told the campground owner she wanted to plant flowers there.

During the trial, spectators learned Ada Peters was born Ada Lamb in Platte Center, Nebraska. The mother of six was first married to Tom Egan, who died in a hunting accident in 1929. She married Robert Peters in 1932 in Kansas City, but he later died, leaving her a widow twice in the middle of the Great Depression.

Ada had a hard time explaining to the jury why Otto did not take the poison himself. She also could not show why she cut Otto up into seven pieces and secretly buried him in two graves next to their cabin. The jury did not believe her and gave her life in prison.

She Was Boiling Mad

November 26, 2011—331 Fairway Drive, Daly City
Murderer: Jesusa Ursula Tatad
Victim: Ronnie Tatad

An immigrant's life is tough. Leaving one's family and friends is a very serious decision for anyone to make. Starting over in a new country, with different customs, laws, and languages is not an easy thing to do. Even if an immigrant has an advanced degree, they often end up with an underpaying job, bad hours, and substandard housing. The American dream brings them here with a chance for a better life, with better opportunities, because in America, if you work hard you will be paid back with a better life. Many immigrates come to America, work five, ten, or twenty years, and go back to their home country with money in their pocket and a more worldly manner to impress the opposite sex.

Daly City is a bedroom community that borders southwestern San Francisco and a half dozen other suburban towns. Daly City was a village until after World War II, when America went into a building boom. While there are pleasant areas of Daly City, with nice houses with views, the majority of the town was erected with claptrap material bought at bargain-basement prices and built at an unnaturally fast speed. By the 1990s, the original apartment buildings that were slapped together in the late 1940s were being replaced with a more modern version of the claptrap apartment. If you are an immigrant working in San Francisco, there is a very good chance you live in Daly City. With rents being some of the most expensive in the world, there are few affordable places for working class people in San Francisco.

Jesusa and Ronnie Tatad, a married couple from the Catanduanes province in the Philippines, lived in Daly City. Ronnie, a registered nurse, worked at Laguna Honda Hospital in San Francisco. They left their two daughters in the care of relatives so they could make a go of it in America, believing that once they were on their feet they would send for their children—but things did not turn out the way they expected. The couple divorced in December 1997, but they still shared their tiny one-room studio apartment at 331 Fairway Drive, along with Ronnie's brother and sister—four adults living in a six-hundred-square-foot studio apartment immigrant-style to save money.

In November 2011, Jesusa walked in on Ronnie having sex with another woman. Even though they were divorced, Ronnie and Jesusa still carried on some type of romantic relationship. Jesusa simmered with anger. When, on the morning of November 26, 2011, Ronnie came home from working the night shift much later than usual, he fell into his bed exhausted and went to sleep.

Jesusa had left her tropical island in the Philippines to start a new life in America. She left her children, parents, and siblings and had nothing to show for all her effort. To add to her loneliness, she only spoke her native Tagalog. Jesusa put on a large pot of water and got it boiling hot. Walking silently to the sleeping thirty-six-year-old, Jesusa threw back the blanket covering Ronnie and dumped the pot of boiling water on her husband. Screaming in pain, Ronnie ran to the bathroom shower, but Jesusa followed him with a baseball bat and hit him with it until Ronnie ran outside to save his life. He ran up Coronado Street for two blocks, half naked and in excruciating pain, until he collapsed in front of a man. Ronnie suffered second and third degree burns. The man called an ambulance. When Jesusa caught up with her husband, he scrambled to get away from her. Jesusa asked the man to cancel his call for an ambulance, but he refused. When police arrived, Ronnie screamed to them, "She burned me! She poured hot water on me!" Jesusa admitted to the crime and was arrested. Paramedics took Ronnie away screaming in agony to San Francisco General Hospital where he died on December 9, 2011, of bacterial blood infection. He had second and third degree burns over 54 percent of his body and had been on a ventilator since being admitted to the hospital.

Jesusa, who was born on Christmas Day, spent her fortieth birthday at the San Mateo County Jail Maguire Correctional Facility in Redwood City, California.

She entered a guilty plea to second-degree murder and was sentenced to sixteen-years-to-life in prison, virtually leaving her nine- and fourteen-year-old daughters orphans back in the Philippines.

Jesusa had left her tropical paradise where she had family, friends, and a relatively uncomplicated life for the damp, chilly climate of San Francisco where she worked menial jobs and lived in an overcrowded slum. She was a mother who left behind two young daughters with the idea that she would bring them to America once they got on their feet. Instead, she is being kept behind bars, seven thousand miles from her home, for at least sixteen years.

It Worked Once Before

June 29, 1985/January 5, 2015—Wilderness Court, Diamond Springs
Murderer: Colleen Harris
Victims: James Batten and Robert Edward Harris

Placerville is a beautiful little town in the foothills of the Sierra Nevada Mountains, forty-five miles east of Sacramento. The county seat of El Dorado County has been around since 1848, when James Marshall discovered gold in nearby Coloma. Originally called Hangtown, the town officially changed its name in 1854. Once the Gold Rush simmered down and hard-rock mining began, Placerville became a supply town and center of law in El Dorado County, which stretches from Folsom Lake, outside of Sacramento, to Lake Tahoe and the Nevada state line.

The huge county has always had a hard-scrabble population of loners who want nothing more than to be left alone, and has a long history of people taking matters into their own hands. In a county where it may take police two hours to get to the scene of a disturbance, rural El Dorado residents often respond to threats by themselves. When a he said/she said situation ends up with only one person alive, and forensic evidence does not prove otherwise, the living goes free.

Colleen Harris worked as a successful professional surveyor in Placerville. Her husband, Robert Edward Harris, was a popular character in Diamond Springs, a small town a couple of miles south of Placerville. A retired U.S. Forest Service supervisor for the extensive Tahoe basin, Bob served as a reserve sheriff deputy, baseball umpire, and globetrotting conservationist. He also helped Colleen with her surveying business. The couple knew each other in high school but both married other people. They eventually married in 1990 after Bob divorced his first wife. He and Colleen divorced in 2004, then remarried in 2005.

By 2014, the second marriage was all but over. Bob moved out and lived alone in a cabin they owned near Lake Tahoe. The seventy-two-year-old volunteered with the Tahoe-Baikal Institute, an international partnership for environmental inquiry, research, and action based in South Lake Tahoe. The Tahoe Baikal Institute works to protect Earth's two deepest fresh water lakes; Tahoe and Lake Baikal in eastern Siberia. He had met a thirty-four-

year-old doctoral candidate while on a research expedition in Mongolia, and began an extremely long-distance love affair with the woman.

Not in the mood to be single at seventy-two years old, Colleen would not accept Bob's new relationship. Bob moved back to the couple's Diamond Springs home to help Colleen while she recovered from hip surgery. He kept in touch with his girlfriend through email and texts, being as discreet as possible to not upset the recovering Colleen.

Colleen knew that her marriage to Bob had disintegrated and was angry that her husband had fallen for a woman old enough to be his grand-daughter. She refused to spend her golden years alone in Diamond Springs while Bob frolicked around the world with a smart, beautiful younger woman. When she discovered Bob had bought his girlfriend a necklace and was texting her, Colleen hit the ceiling.

On January 5, 2015, while Bob slept, Colleen walked into their bedroom with a 12-gauge shotgun. Putting the end of the barrel right up against Bob's left ear, she fired and blew Bob's face into his pillow. Colleen casually wiped the blood splatter from the wall and cleaned up brain matter and flesh off the sheets.

Bob's adult children grew concerned when he did not answer any of the text messages they sent him that day. They called the police for a welfare visit. When police arrived at her home, they found Colleen washing dishes. She told them she killed Bob in self-defense because he was violent and she was tired of his physical and emotional abuse. This marked the beginning of Colleen Harris's "gray fog" memory of the crime, but there was no "gray fog" clouding the memories of law officials and neighbors who remembered a similar incident Colleen underwent thirty years earlier.

In 1985, Colleen was married to husband number two, James Batten, and they lived in the same home on Wilderness Court, a short forested lane of half a dozen homes just off Pleasant Valley Road. On June 29, 1985, Colleen shot James with a .410-caliber shotgun as he sat on their bed reading the newspaper. Just to make sure that he was dead, she fired another shell into him at close range. So there would be no mistake of self-defense, Colleen planted a pistol at Batten's side. At Colleen's trial, her daughter from her first marriage, Tawnie Black, told the jury that she had allegedly been mentally, physically, and sexually victimized by Batten for years. It was convenient for Colleen that Batten was dead and could not defend himself against the charges. A jury acquitted Colleen Batten and let her back into society, where thirty years later she killed again.

The second time, Colleen had a much harder time explaining what happened. Investigators did not take her alleged "gray fog" seriously, as she had told conflicting stories about how Bob died. First it was suicide, then self-defense, then an accident.

The defense introduced cell phone records indicating Colleen drove to San Francisco around seven in the morning the day after the murder. She went there to leave Bob's coin collection and a pistol with his son for safe keeping.

The prosecution played a telephone recording of Colleen cheerfully calling an auto club for roadside assistance on the way back from San Francisco. Her car had stalled near Davis on Interstate 80 in the early afternoon. Once she realized that her vehicle was fine, she telephoned the road service and canceled the call, laughing as she explained that her car was fine.

The prosecution displayed phone records indicating Colleen called her attorney around 3 p.m. and then ditched Bob's cell phone about twenty miles from her home. Not exactly the behavior of someone who had just witnessed a suicide.

Helping the prosecution's case was Bob's daughter, Los Angeles police detective Pam Stirling. Detective Stirling had received an angry text message from Colleen about Bob speaking to his faraway girlfriend. The detective told the jury that her father had recently told her he was afraid of Colleen.

Colleen's daughter, Tawnie Black was called by the defense to testify about the abuse Colleen suffered at the hands of her step-father, James Batten, but during cross-examination she admitted she had taken out a restraining order on her mother two years ago in 2013. In the restraining order, Black declared she had once seen her mother pull a pistol on her father, Colleen's first husband Larry Dodge, and that she was afraid of her.

A forensic scientist called by the prosecution put the final nails in the case when he proved Bob could not have held the gun and shot himself in the direction of the wound and the position of his body.

On April 15, 2015, the jury came back with a guilty verdict after deliberating for only two hours. Colleen Harris was sentenced to fifty years to life.

Bibliography

BOOKS

Braidhill, Kathy. *To Die For: The Shocking True Story of Female Serial Killer Dana Sue Gray*. New York: St. Martin's Press, 2000

Smith, Carlton. *Cold-Blooded: A True Story of Love, Lies, Greed, and Murder*. New York: St. Martin's Press, 2004

Thomas, Mike. *You Might Remember Me: The Life and Times of Phil Hartman*. New York: St. Martin's Press, 2014

NEWSPAPERS

AB Kvällstidningen Expressen
The American River Current
Associated Press
Bay City News
Beckström Kommunalarbetaren
Bluefield Daily Telegraph
Expressen
Fresno Bee
Gefle Dagblad
Inland Valley Daily Bulletin
LA Weekly
Lake County News
The Local
Los Angeles Times
Los Angeles Daily News
Mountain Democrat
News-Sentinel
New York Daily News
Oakland Tribune
Orange County Register

OC Weekly
The Palm Beach Post
Riverside Press-Enterprise
Sacramento Bee
Sacramento Union
Santa Barbara Independent
San Bernardino County Sun
Swedish Dagbladet
St. Petersburg Times
San Francisco Chronicle
San Jose MercuryNews
Santa Ana Orange County Register
The Times of Oman
Västerbottens Folkblad
Whittier Daily News
Winnipeg Free Press

MAGAZINES

People
The New Yorker
Time Magazine

WEBSITES

www.annikaostberg.se
CBS San Francisco
CBS13
CNN
Deranged L.A. Crimes
Huffington Post
Journal Group Link International
Jim Fisher True Crime blog
Ktla.com
Murderpedia

Newsvine
NBCsandiego.com
News92fm
Newspaper Archives
Recordnet
Slate
Solon.com
Sgvtribune.com
TrueTv
Utsandiego.com
Death Penalty Information Center

Index

ABOUT THE AUTHOR

David Kulczyk (pronounced Coal-check) is a Sacramento-based California crime historian. He was born in Bay City, Michigan, in 1958, and grew up in nearby Linwood. He spent his twenties as a musician, his thirties as a bike messenger, his forties making money, and his fifties writing books. His work has appeared in *The San Francisco Bay Guardian, The East Bay Express, Madison Magazine, Maximum Ink Music Magazine, Pop Culture Press, The Seattle Times* and *The Sacramento News and Review.* Kulczyk has written three other books, *California Justice: Shootouts, Lynchings and Assassinations in the Golden State; Death In California: The Bizarre, Freakish, and Just Curious Ways People Die in the Golden State;* and *California's Fruits, Flakes and Nuts: True Tales of California Crazies, Crackpots and Creeps.* He has a B.A. in History from California State University, Sacramento.

ABOUT THE ILLUSTRATOR

Freelance Illustrator Olaf Jens was born on January 19, 1965, in Vlijmen, The Netherlands. He studied art at Artibus in Utrecht, and at the Koninklijke Academie voor Kunst en Vormgeving in Den Bosch, The Netherlands. Over the years his work has graced in various magazines, newspapers, posters, and LPs on Crypt, Sellwood, Amok, Coffee Addict, Southern Routes, Trailer Park, and Slovenly Records. He currently lives in Grass Valley, California.

More by David Kulczyk

$15.95
($17.95 Canada)

California Justice

Shootouts, Lynchings, and Assassinations in the Golden State

by David Kulczyk

In the movies, vigilante justice is clean and neat, a simple case of good guys defeating bad guys. In real history, justice is never so black and white. Sometimes it is difficult to tell the victims from the perpetrators. From the Oregon-California line to the Mexican border; from an 1850 squatter's riot to a bloody 2003 confrontation at a Ukiah Wal-Mart, David Kulczyk probes California's most notorious shootouts, lynchings, and assassinations.

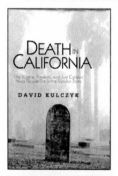

$15.95
($17.95 Canada)

Death in California

The Bizarre, Freakish, and Just Curious Ways People Die in the Golden State

by David Kulczyk

Death in California chronicles 31 bizarre and grisly true stories, from a jet crashing into a Bay Area kitchen to the actor who discovered the absolutely dumbest way to light a cigarette—a cheerfully perverse history of murders, accidents, overdoses, suicides, and fatal stupidity. Brutally funny, haunting, and poignant, this zany collection is delightfully weird and enthrallingly human.

$14.95
($16.95 Canada)

California Fruits, Flakes and Nuts

True Tales of California Crazies, Crackpots, and Creeps

by David Kulczyk

A freewheeling catalog of misfits, eccentrics, creeps, criminals and failed dreamers, **California Fruits, Flakes and Nuts** relates the hilarious and heartbreaking lives of 48 bizarre personalities who exemplify California's well-deserved reputation for nonconformity. It's a side-splitting, shocking, and salacious salute to the people who made California the strangest place on earth.

Available from bookstores, online bookstores, and CravenStreetBooks.com, or by calling toll-free 1-800-345-4447.

Secrets of California History

When San Francisco Burned

A Photographic Memoir of the Great San Francisco Earthquake and Fire of 1906

by Douglas L. Gist

When San Francisco Burned presents for the first time raw, candid photographs of the Great San Francisco Earthquake and Fire of 1906. These amazingly detailed and dramatic photographs show the earthquake and its aftermath from a street-level perspective, giving readers an unprecedented look at what it was really like to be in San Francisco during those terrible days.

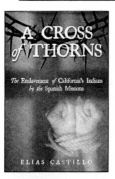

$21.95
($23.95 Canada)

A Cross of Thorns

The Enslavement of California's Indians by the Spanish Missions

by Elias Castillo

Despite their whitewashed image, the California Missions were places of enslavement, physical punishment, and deliberate cruelty. **A Cross of Thorns** presents the facts of the Spanish occupation of California, citing Spanish church and government archives, contemporary accounts of mission life, and the letters of Junípero Serra, who declared that "blows" were the only way to "civilize" Indians.

$19.95
($20.95 Canada)

Pardon My Hearse

A Colorful Portrait of Where the Funeral and Entertainment Industries Met in Hollywood

by Allan Abbott & Greg Abbott

In **Pardon My Hearse**, Allan Abbott tells the rags-to-shroud story of how we went from a young man with a hearse to the funeral director to the stars, including the secrets of the funerals of Marilyn Monroe, Natalie Wood, and more—a rollicking, hilarious story of eye-opening revelations of secret Hollywood from the man who literally knows where the bodies are buried.

$16.95
($17.95 Canada)

New Books on the West

Walking San Francisco's 49 Mile Scenic Drive

Explore the Famous Sites, Neighborhoods, and Vistas in 17 Enchanting Walks

by Kristine Poggioli and Carolyn Eidson

$16.95
($21.95 Canada)

Walking San Francisco's 49 Mile Scenic Drive takes you the length of the famous 49 Mile Drive in 17 bite-size walks, complete with turn-by-turn instructions, maps, and historical facts—a perfect guidebook for today's urban enthusiast who values walkable neighborhoods, hyperlocal culture, and the pleasure of walking..

Choose Your Weapon

The Duel in California, 1847–1861

by Christopher Burchfield

$16.95
($21.95 Canada)

In Gold Rush California, armed thugs shot at each other in the streets—and in the 1850s, the thugs were prominent journalists, state legislators, governors, and even the Chief Justice of the state Supreme Court. **Choose Your Weapon** describes in graphic detail the personalities, issues, weapons, and violence that marked the golden age of dueling in California, revealing a wild and dangerous history of politics in the Golden State.

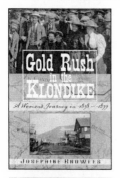

Gold Rush in the Klondike

A Woman's Journey in 1898–1899

by Josephine Knowles

$22.95
($28.95 Canada)

Never before published, **Gold Rush in the Klondike** is Josephine Knowles' personal memoir of day-to-day life in the height of the Klondike Gold Rush. A Victorian gentlewoman of refinement, Knowles endured cold, disease, and malnutrition, and won the friendship and trust of the miners for her stoicism, courage, and compassion. Knowles presents terrifying struggles against a hostile environment, picturesque descriptions of an untouched Arctic wilderness and keen observations of men and women on the frontier.

Available from bookstores, online bookstores, and
CravenStreetBooks.com, or by calling toll-free 1-800-345-4447.

CPSIA information can be obtained
at www.ICGtesting.com
Printed in the USA
LVOW12s0023011217
558246LV00001B/115/P